Small
Amish Quilt
Patterns

Small
Amish Quilt
Patterns

Rachel T. Pellman

Good Books

Intercourse, Pennsylvania 17534

Acknowledgments

Designed and illustrated by Craig N. Heisey.
We wish to give special thanks to the following persons for their gracious permission to picture their quilts on the covers of this book:
Front cover, clockwise from top left—Sunshine and Shadow in a Diamond, Dr. and Mrs. Donald Herr; Bow Ties, collection of Eve and David Wheatcroft, Lewisburg, PA.; Lone Star, Pat and Kemp Beall; Bear Paw, Pat and Kemp Beall; Log Cabin, collection of Eve and David Wheatcroft, Lewisburg, PA.; Nine-Patch, collection of Eve and David Wheatcroft, Lewisburg, PA.; Rolling Stone, Pat and Kemp Beall. Back cover—Sunshine and Shadow, Dr. and Mrs. Donald Herr.

Photograph Credits

Photos on covers and on pages 7, 13, and 126 by Kirk Zutell/BRT Photographic Illustrations.

Small Amish Quilt Patterns

Table of Contents

Small Amish Quilt Patterns	6
Total Quilt Assembly Diagram	14
Border Application Diagram	15
Center Diamond	16
Sunshine and Shadow	18
Bars	20
Multiple Patch	22
Irish Chain	24
Log Cabin	26
Rail Fence	29
Double T	30
Stars	32
Jacob's Ladder	34
Baskets	36
Fan	38
Ocean Waves	40
Roman Stripe	42
Tumbling Blocks	44
Bow Tie	46
Robbing Peter to Pay Paul	48
Shoo-Fly	50
Crown of Thorns	51
Monkey Wrench	52
Carolina Lily	54
Bear Paw	56
Pinwheel	58
Garden Maze	60
Railroad Crossing	62
Double Wedding Ring	64
Diagonal Triangles	67
Drunkard's Path	68
Tree of Life	70
Bachelor's Puzzle	72
Rolling Stone	74
Quilting Templates	76
Circular Feather	77
Triangular Rose	79
Floral Corner A	81
Feather Border	83
Floral Corner B	87
Ivy Leaf	87
Fiddlehead Fern	89
Floral Corner C	91
Tulip A	93
Cable A	93
Cable B	95
Tulip B	97
Grapes with Leaves	97
Pumpkin Seed	99
Floral Border Design	99
Dogwood	99
Fan A	101
Basket with Tulip	101
Leaves	103
Fruit	105
Floral Corner D	105
Baskets	107
Feather Heart with Cross-Hatching	109
Fan B	111
Diamond	111
Floral Corner E	113
Scalloped Border	115
Clamshell	117
Squares	119
Hearts	123
Readings and Sources	125
Index	127
About the Author	128

Small Amish Quilt Patterns

Antique Amish crib quilts are avidly sought by collectors of Amish crafts. When found, these small treasures bring prices close to, or exceeding, full-sized quilts of the same genre.

The reasons for the high values placed on these small quilts are varied. First, these bedcovers are scarce. Fewer crib quilts were made to supply the needs of a household. A quilt could be made for the crib and remain as the crib cover for a series of different occupants. Obviously, such a quilt went through repeated washings. Often they were used until they were thoroughly worn and then thrown out and replaced. Today, collectors are often willing to pay high prices for a crib quilt even if it shows severe signs of wear.

Secondly, crib quilts are desirable because of their size. They make magnificent wall displays and are more likely than larger quilts to fit on the wall spaces of modern homes.

Then there is the special feeling connected with crib quilts. They stand as a tangible symbol of love and caring. They hold warm memories of childhood, carefree days, and restful nights, the secure feelings of loving and being loved.

Small Amish Quilt Patterns provides the patterns to create these treasures anew. Patterns have been reduced in size so that the proportions will be pleasing in a small quilt. Templates for piecing, as well as quilting designs, are given in actual size so that no adaptation is required on the part of the maker. Though they are suitable for crib quilts, these patterns should not be limited to that. They make dynamic wallhangings and can be custom-designed to suit both color and space requirements.

When used as wallhangings, these quilts are truly display pieces and can be painstakingly pieced and quilted without fear of the wear and tear of normal use. Or what better gift can be given than a handmade quilt to cuddle and comfort a child through the dark night hours!

Lone Star, 1937. Cotton, 39 × 49. Thomas, Oklahoma. Pat and Kemp Beall.

Choosing a pattern

Amish crib quilts are made in a wide variety of patterns. And many patterns look "Amish" because of the colors used. The three designs that are distinctively Amish are the Center Diamond, Sunshine and Shadow, and Bars patterns. These, by virtue of their simplicity and straight lines, are easy to piece and therefore excellent choices for beginners. However, a trademark of these patterns is also their elaborate quilting designs, so to recreate them requires the patience and skill to cover them with tiny even quilting stitches.

A beginning quilter will be less frustrated by choosing a pattern that can be assembled in straight line units rather than one that requires setting in triangles. For example, the Nine-patch pattern can be done in a series of straight lines, whereas the Lone Star quilt requires setting a triangle piece into a corner. Study the assembly instructions of a pattern and choose one that provides an adequate challenge without undue difficulty.

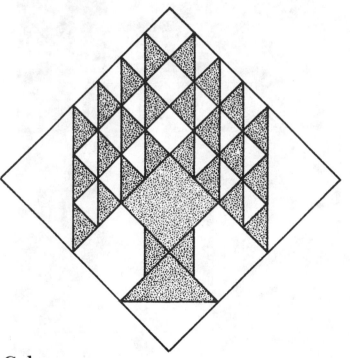

Color

Probably the most distinctive element of small Amish quilts is their color. Like full-sized Amish quilts, the smaller versions employ the bold, deep, solid colors of Amish clothing. Pastels are *not* the norm for Amish crib quilts. These quilts are vibrant pieces that dance with rich, full hues.

Predominant colors in Amish quilts are those ranging from dark red to, and including, green on the color wheel. These colors tend to be the ones a woman would use for her family's clothing. The scraps make delightful quilts. Since blacks and browns are often part of the Amish palette, these also appear in quilts. The effect of these neutral colors is to highlight the other fabrics.

Since Amish women did not study color theory, the energy of their quilts is likely the result of truly uninhibited color combinations. In today's American society where clothing, home furnishings and offices are all carefully planned and color-coordinated, it is difficult for the modern quilter to "forget" what goes together and play freely with color.

When planning your colors, it may be helpful to do a small scale model of the full quilt on graph paper and color it with colored pencils to see what the overall effect will be. Better yet, cut small pieces of actual fabric and glue them onto paper to get an accurate color representation.

Since printed fabrics are not used, contrast is achieved only by varying color hues and shades. To make a patchwork design stand out sharply, it must be contrasted against a different color or be set against a lighter or darker background. For more subtle variations the contrasts need not be strong. However, there should always be adequate contrast for the pattern to be clear, or the quilt top will look muddled and undefined.

Color is relative and is affected by its surroundings. Therefore final fabric selections need to be made with all the options together. A color that looks bright by itself may be dull next to other fabrics. Also, adding touches of black may serve to highlight and pick up an otherwise dull quilt. Experiment with color. Play with options before making a final decision.

Buying Fabric

The quality of a finished quilt depends on the quality of its individual components. So it is worth the investment to buy high quality fabrics. Cotton and cotton polyester blend fabrics are generally best for quilting. One hundred percent cotton has a dull finish which looks more like the old quilts than the cotton-poly blends which tend to have a bit of sheen. Fabrics should be tightly woven and be lightweight enough to quilt easily through double layers. Fabrics that are slippery and those which fray excessively when cut are not suitable for quilting. As small pieces they are frustrating to sew together and tend to pull apart at the seams.

Yardage

The quilt backing is the single largest fabric requirement. The second largest piece is likely for the borders. It is best to have the borders run the full length of the quilt without piecing them. Therefore, fabric should be purchased with that in mind. Borders can be cut lengthwise in the fabric and patches

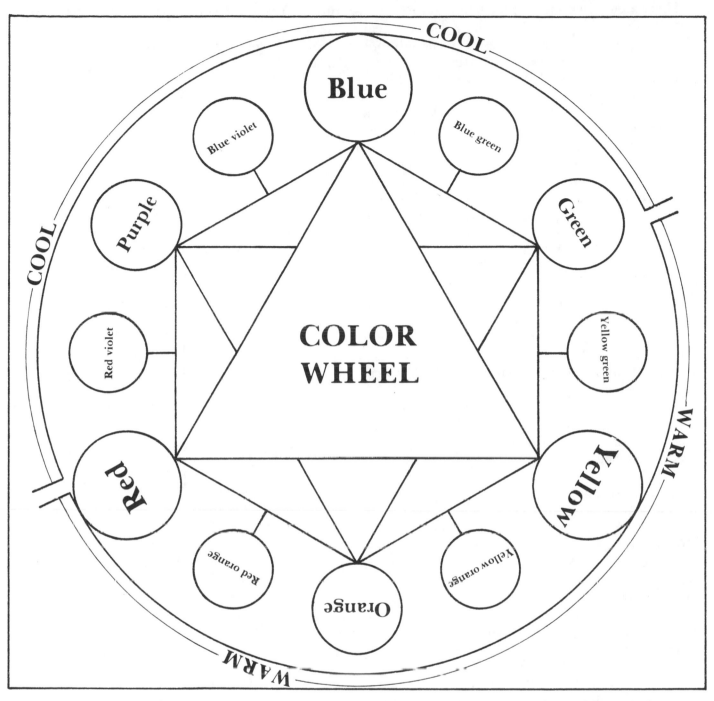

Blue

Blue violet

Blue green

Purple

Green

COOL

COOL

Red violet

Yellow green

COLOR
WHEEL

Red

Yellow

WARM

Red orange

Yellow orange

Orange

WARM

can be cut from remaining edges.

When buying fabric, it is better to buy extra than to run short. Extra yardage can be used for pillows or other accessory items, but it is not always possible to match a color that has been purchased in too short an amount.

Making Templates

Precision is extemely important in quiltmaking and it begins with making templates. Templates for marking fabric must be traced exactly as they are on the pattern. They should be made of some durable material that will not wear down with repeated tracings. Plastic lids, plastic milk cartons or bleach bottles are an excellent source of template material. Make

the template, then glue a piece of fine sandpaper to one side. When laid on the fabric the sandpaper prevents slippage and is more conducive to accurate marking. Before marking and cutting all the patches, sew one unit together to test the pattern. If it fits perfectly, proceed with the marking. If not, re check the template and make necessary alterations.

Marking Quilt Patches

There are many varieties of fabric-marking pencils available to quilters. Each has its assets. Before using any pencil or pen, test it on the fabric to be sure it provides a line that is clear and precise. A regular lead pencil will work on many fabrics.

There are two ways to mark patches—with or without the seam allowance. If marking with the seam allowance, the template is made large enough to include the seam allowance. The template is then traced, and the fabric cut and sewn ¼ inch inside the cut edge.

When marking without the seam allowance, the template is made the actual size of the finished piece. The cutting is then done ¼ inch outside the marked line. The marked line thus serves as a sewing guide. The advantage to this method is that each patch has lines, guaranteeing accurate piecing. The disadvantage is that each patch must be marked individually and cut individually. Try both methods and stick with the one that feels most comfortable.

Piecing

If the pieces have been cut and marked accurately, piecing the quilt is rewarding and fun. Piecing can be done by hand or by machine. Machine piecing is a great deal faster and in many cases makes a stronger seam. However, it is difficult to be as precise with a machine, especially with tiny pieces. When hand piecing, the stitch is a tiny running stitch, reinforced occasionally with a backstitch. Care must be taken to keep the seam taut, but not so tight as to cause puckering.

Whether piecing by hand or by machine, follow assembly instructions so that all patches are built in straight seam units whenever possible. When corners must be set in they can be done either by stitching from the outer edge of the patch to the corner (stopping at the seam allowance), pivoting, and sewing out to the other edge, or by starting at the corner, sewing one edge, and then returning to the corner and sewing the other edge. Practice both methods and choose the one most easily executed.

When machine piecing, it is most efficient to stack patches in order and sew all like units at once. For example, when making a Log Cabin, sew all the center squares to the first log section, then add all #2 logs, etc. When sewing the patches, do not clip threads between each unit. Rather, feed them through the machine in a continuous row and clip them at the end of a section (ie, there is no need to clip threads between each "square plus log" unit of the log cabin). Rather, sew all of them and clip them apart before adding log #2, repeating the same procedure for log #3.

It is generally best to lay all seam allowances in one direction. Exceptions to this rule are when a dark fabric is next to a light fabric and the seam allowance would show through the light fabric if laid in that direction. A second exception applies when seam allowances would interfere with quilting if laid in one

direction. If these situations exist it is best to hide or avoid having to quilt through the allowance even if it means they must be laid opposite from other allowances.

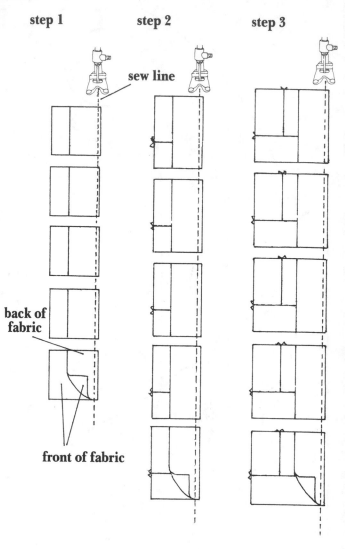

Marking and Quilting

Antique Amish quilts stand apart with their generous and lovely quilting. Quilting designs should be full and stitches should be tiny and even. Quilt-marking pencils are the same as those used for marking cutting lines. However, remember that quilting lines are marked directly on the surface of the quilt and will not be hidden by the quilting threads. Therefore, the lines must be light or removable.

When working with fabrics that are light enough to see through, the easiest method of marking is to trace the quilting design. This is done by outlining the quilting motif on paper with a heavy marker. Lay the quilt top, right side up, on top of the design and simply trace the design on to the fabric. If the fabric is too dark for that method, a template must be made to lay on top of the fabric and traced through. This can be done by cutting thin slashes periodically on the quilting template lines so a marker point can fit through and trace the pattern. Some types of transfer marking paper are suitable but the lines must be able to be easily removed after quilting is completed.

After the quilt top is marked with its quilting lines, it is ready for the actual stitching process. The purpose of quilting is to hold together the three layers which constitute the actual quilt—the back, batting, and top.

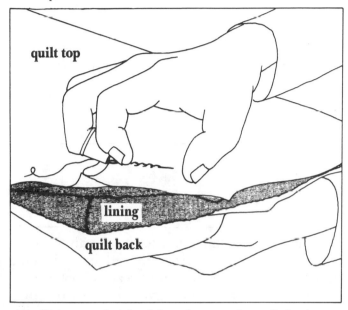

A quilt is a sandwich of three layers—the quilt back, lining or batting, and the quilt top—all held together by the quilting stitches.

The type of batting chosen will affect the overall look of the quilt. A polyester batt will give a full puffy quality to the quilted lines. Cotton batting will be a bit flatter and should be quilted more closely to prevent lumpiness when the quilt is washed. Another option is to use a piece of cotton flannel or an old blanket which will give a flat appearance much like the antique quilts.

Whatever type is chosen, the three layers of the quilt must be stretched and held together throughout the quilting process. Large quilts are generally stretched in a frame for quilting. Small quilts are easily done in the same manner. However, smaller quilts can be done without the use of a large frame. The important thing is that all three layers be stretched flat and basted together before quilting. To achieve this, lay the quilt back on a large flat surface. Cover it with the batting and finally the quilt top. Pin the three layers together. Beginning in the center and working out to the edge, baste the entire quilt in 5 to 8 inch intervals. (The basting must be removed after the quilting is done so avoid quilting over the basting as much as possible.) Remove the pins and

the "sandwich" is ready for quilting.

Quilting is simple running stitch. Stitches need to be tight but not so tight as to cause puckering. Quilting is done with a single thickness of special quilting thread. To begin, the knot is gently pulled through the fabric so it is hidden in the batting layer of the quilt.

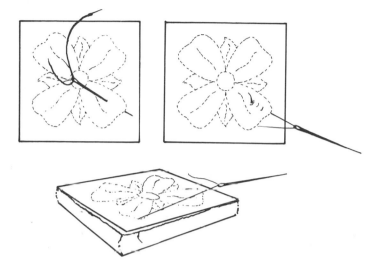

To both secure the quilting thread at the beginning and hide the knot, insert the needle through only the quilt top about 1 inch from where the quilting will begin, pull the thread through to the knot, and gently tug on the knot until it slips through the fabric and is lodged invisibly underneath the top.

Quilting needles are called "betweens" and are shorter than regular hand sewing needles. The higher the number, the finer the needle. Many quilters prefer using a size 8 or 9 needle. A thimble is needed to push the needle through all the layers.

The quilter's one hand should be underneath the quilt to feel when the needle has successfully penetrated the three layers and to help guide the needle upward again. The upper hand receives the needle and pushes it back down. About five stitches can be stacked on the needle before the length of thread is pulled through. When working small curves only two or three stitches can be stacked at a time.

When the length of thread is used, make a tiny backstitch and reinsert the needle through only the top layer. Take a long stitch, pull the needle out, and clip the thread. The goal in quilting is tiny even stitches. Practice seems to be the best teacher.

Binding

The final step in completing a quilt is the binding. This finishes the raw edges. Binding can be done by wrapping some of the quilt backing around to the front, wrapping the front to the back, or by adding a binding strip. Adding a binding strip is probably the

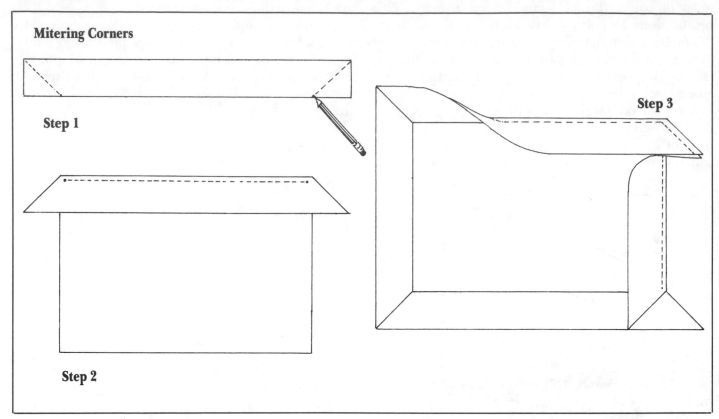

Mitering Corners

Step 1

Step 2

Step 3

most durable since it can be done in a double thickness. To do so, cut two strips of fabric the width of the quilt and about three to four inches wide. Fold this in half, wrong sides together. Pin it to the top and bottom edge of the quilt top, right sides together, with the fold facing the center of the quilt and raw edges of the binding and quilt aligned. Stitch this in place. Cut two more strips the length of the quilt, plus the extended binding, plus one inch on each end. Sew these on in the same manner, being sure to have the top and bottom binding fully extended. Wrap the binding around to the back of the quilt, placing the fold of the binding along the seam line. Handstitch the binding in place, folding in corners.

Mitering Borders

There are times when the appearance of a border is greatly enhanced by mitering rather than using straight edges. This is especially true of the quilt that has a double, triple, or striped border.

Measure length of quilt top. Add border width × 2. For example, if the length of the quilt is 60 inches and the border is 5 inches wide, you will cut the border to be 70 inches or 60 plus 5 × 2.

On the right side of each border piece, measure in from each end the exact number of inches as the border width. Using a straight edge, draw a diagonal line from that point to the outer corner. Cut along the angled line (Step 1).

With right sides together, stitch border to quilt top, leaving ¼ inch seam allowance open at each end.

Continue with remaining border pieces, always stopping stitching ¼ inch from the edge, and being careful not to sew through the already attached border piece(s). (If you have sewn correctly, the final stitches on the long sides and short sides will meet at each corner.) (Step 2).

Finally, open border pieces and with their right sides together, sew corner seams. The ¼ inch seam allowance left open at ends of each border will now be used as the seam allowance on the mitered corner. Stitch from inside corner to outside edge. Backstitch to secure seams at ends (Step 3).

If desired, bindings may be mitered in the same way.

To Display Quilts

Wall quilts can be hung in various ways. One is to simply tack the quilt directly to the wall. However, this is potentially damaging to both quilt and wall, and unless it is a permanent hanging, it is probably not the best way. Another option is to hang the quilt like a painting. To do so, make narrow sleeve from matching fabric and hand sew it to the upper edge of the quilt along the bace. Insert a dowel rod through the sleeve and hang the rod by wire or nylon string.

The quilt can also be hung on a frame. This method requires velcro or fabric to be attached to the frame itself. In case of velcro, one side of it is stapled to the frame. The opposite velcro is hand-sewn on the edges of the quilt and attached carefully to the velcro on the frame. If fabric is attached to the frame, the quilt is then handstitched to the frame itself. Quilts can also be mounted inside plexiglass by a professional framery. This method, often reserved for antique quilts, can provide an acid free, dirt free and, with special plexiglass, a sun-proof environment for your quilt.

Variations

These pattterns are provided for the sizes specified. However, there is great room for variation. If you want a longer quilt, add a row of patches on the top or bottom. If you need a wider quilt, add patches along each side. Border treatments may vary. The borders are meant to frame the quilt and as long as proper proportions are maintained they may be pieced in various ways.

The patches are also adaptable for pillows. A grouping of patches may be used together or a single patch can be used and enlarged with the use of borders. Pillows can be finished with piping or ruffles or left plain. Quilt patches can also be used to make potholders, placemats, tablerunners and tablecloths and other craft projects. The only limit is your own imagination.

Log Cabin, c. 1900. Cotton and wool, 31 × 42. Holmes Co., Ohio. Collection of Eve and David Wheatcroft, Lewisburg, PA.

13

Total Quilt Assembly Diagram

Diagram 5.

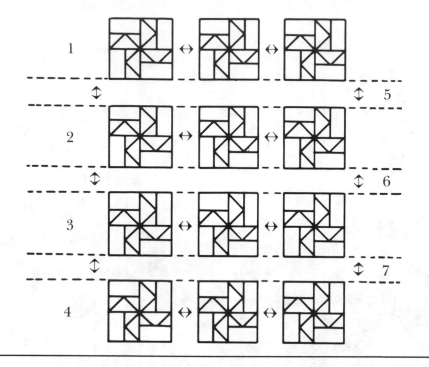

Diagram 6.

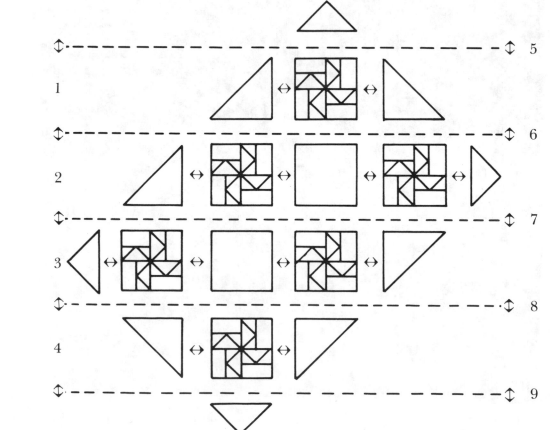

Border Application Diagram

To obtain correct border length, measure length of edge to which border will be applied. Border widths are given with each pattern. When corner blocks are used, sew them to the ends of the last border pieces and then add the border and blocks as a complete section.

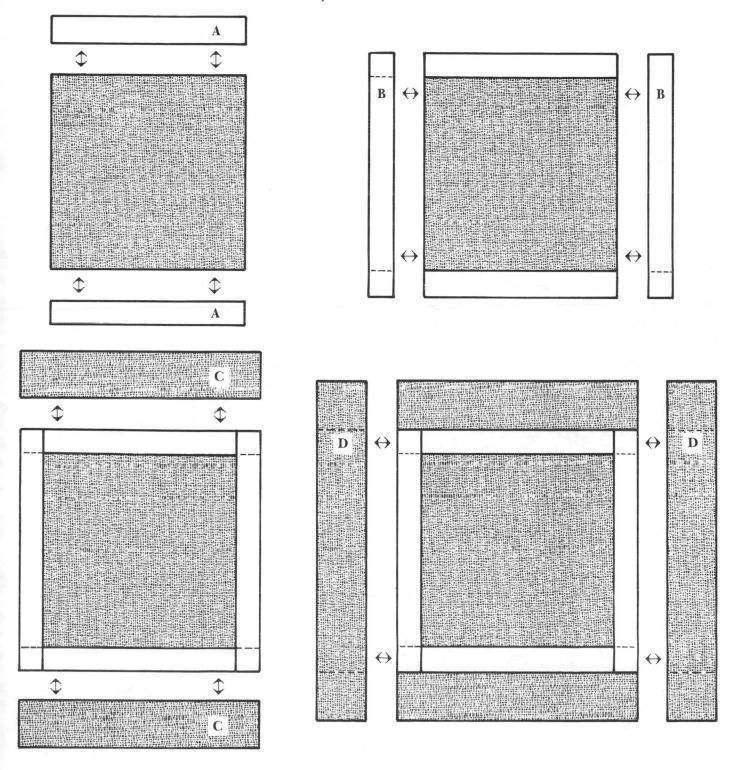

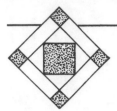

Center Diamond

Variation 1

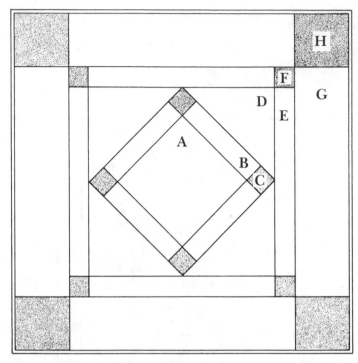

Variation 2

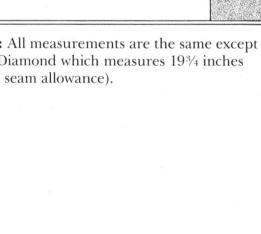

Measurements given <u>without</u> seam allowance

A — 13¾ inches square
B — 13¾ inches by 3 inches
C — 3 inches square
D —

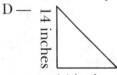

14 inches (vertical) / 14 inches (horizontal)

E — 3 inches by 28 inches
F — 3 inches square
G — 8 inches by 34 inches
H — 8 inches square

Variation 2: All measurements are the same except for Center Diamond which measures 19¾ inches square (add seam allowance).

Assembly instructions:

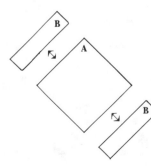

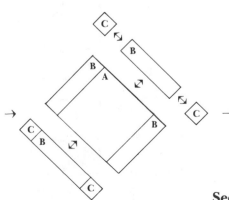

See border Application Diagram, pg. 15.

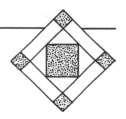

Variation 3—Sawtooth Diamond   Approximate size 48 x 48

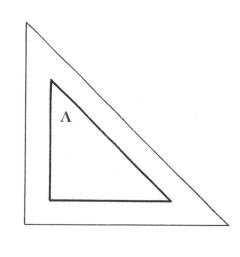

Measurements given <u>without</u> seam allowance

A — triangle template given
B — 6¼ inches square
C — 2½ inches by 8¾ inches
D — 2½ inches by 13¾ inches
E —

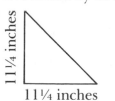
11¼ inches
11¼ inches

F — 2½ inches by 25 inches
G — 2½ inches by 30 inches
H— 8 inches by 32½ inches
I — 8 inches by 48½ inches

Assembly instructions:

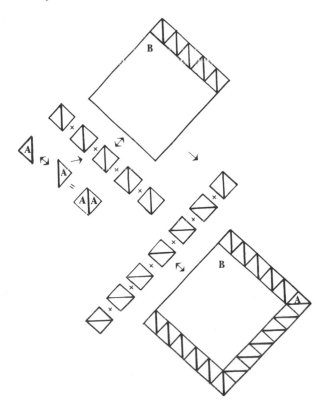

See Border Application Diagram, pg. 15.

Sunshine and Shadow
Approximate size 50 x 50

Variation 1

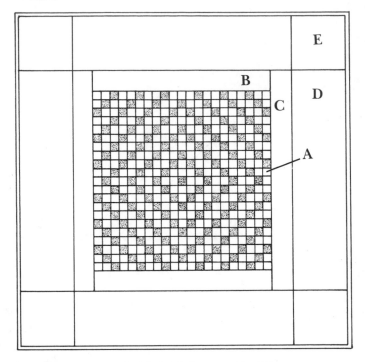

Variation 2—Center Diamond

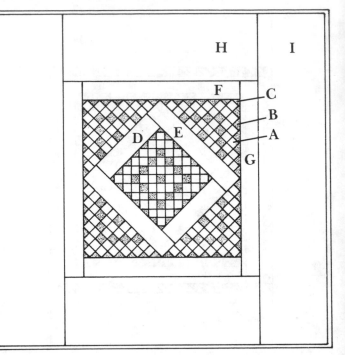

Measurements given <u>without</u> seam allowance

A — square template given
B — 26¼ inches by 3 inches
C — 32¼ inches by 3 inches
D — 32¼ inches by 8 inches
E — 8 inches square

Measurements given <u>without</u> seam allowance

A — square template given
B — triangle template given
C — triangle template given
D — 2¾ inches by 10⅝ inches
E — 2¾ inches by 16¼ inches
F — 2¾ inches by 26½ inches
G — 2¾ inches by 32 inches
H — 8 inches by 32 inches
I — 8 inches by 48 inches

Assembly instructions:

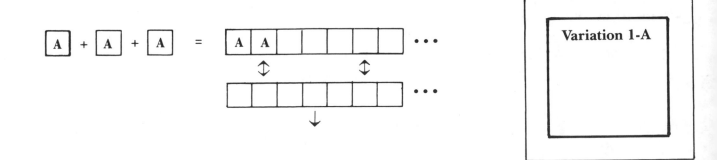

See Border Application Diagram, pg. 15.

Variation 3

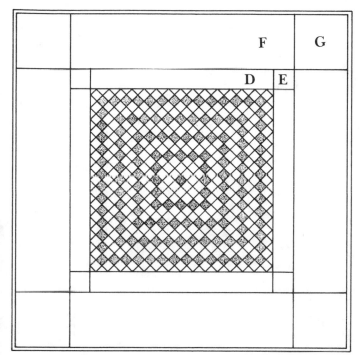

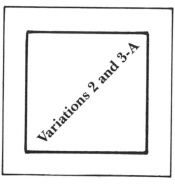

Measurements given <u>without</u> seam allowance

A — square template given
B — triangle template given
C — triangle template given
D — 3 inches x 26¼ inches
E — 3 inches square
F — 8 inches x 32¼
G — 8 inches square

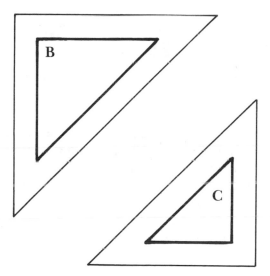

Assembly instructions:

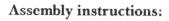

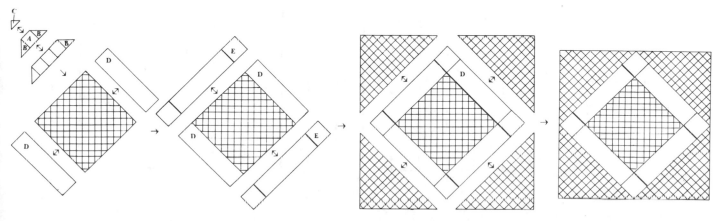

See Border Application Diagram, pg. 15.

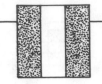

Bars
Approximate size 48 x 48

Variation 1

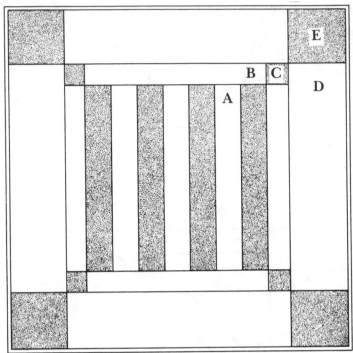

Variation 2

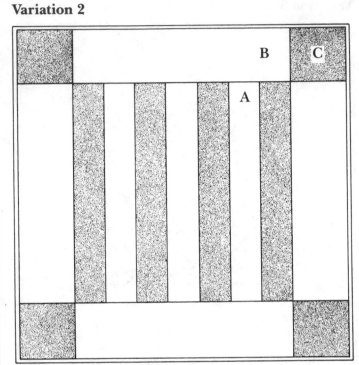

Measurements given <u>without</u> seam allowance

A — 3¾ inches by 26¼ inches
B — 3 inches by 26¼ inches
C — 3 inches square
D — 8 inches by 32½ inches
E — 8 inches square

Measurements given <u>without</u> seam allowance

A — 4½ inches by 31½ inches
B — 8 inches by 31½ inches
C — 8 inches square

Assembly instructions:

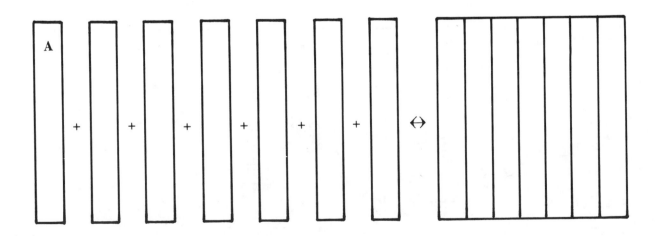

See Border Application Diagram, pg. 15.

Wild Goose Chase Variation   Approximate size 43½ x 58

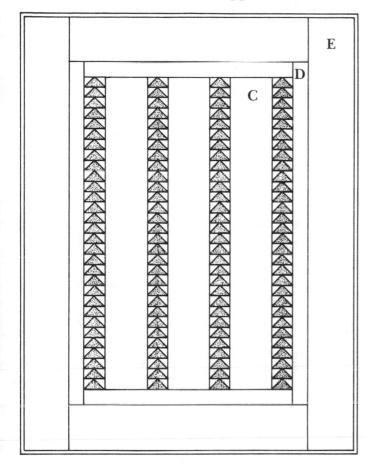

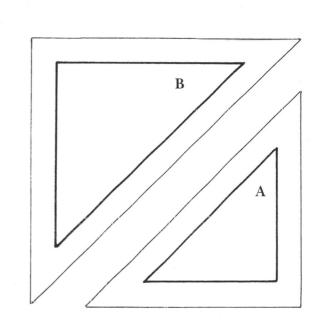

Measurements given <u>without</u> seam allowance
A — triangle template given
B — triangle template given
C — 5½ inches by length of pieced strips
D — 2 inches by width of pieced interior
E — width of outer border 6 inches

Assembly instructions:

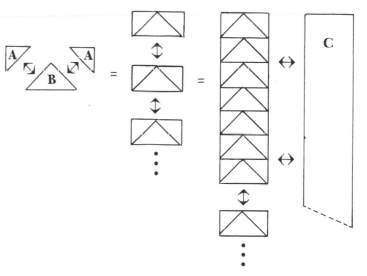

See Border Application Diagram, pg. 15.

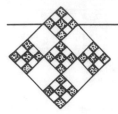

Multiple Patch
Approximate size 46 x 58

Variation 1—Double 9-Patch

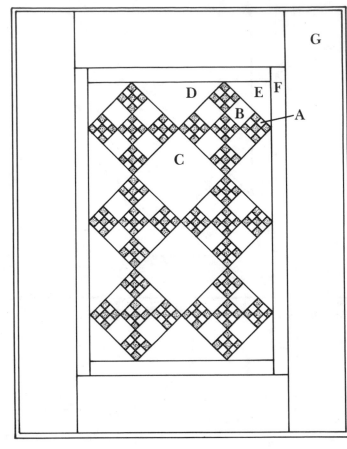

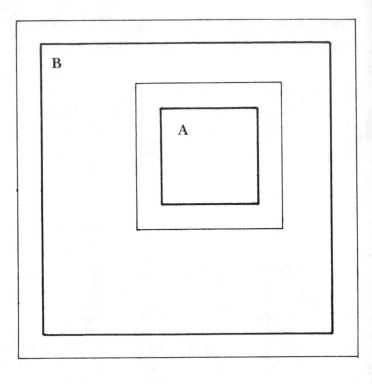

Measurements given <u>without</u> seam allowance

A — template given
B — template given
C — cut 2–9 inch squares
D — cut 6 triangles

E — cut 4 triangles

F — width of inner border 3 inches
G — width of outer border 8 inches

Make 6 pieced blocks

Assembly instructions:

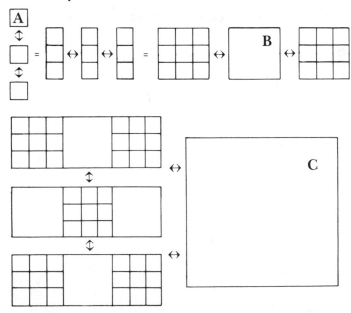

See Diagram 6, pg. 14 (Total Quilts Assembly).
See Border Application Diagram, pg. 15.

Variation 2—Double 4-Patch

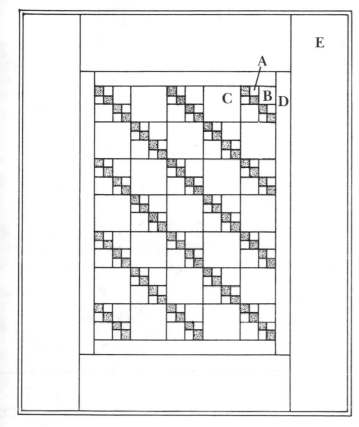

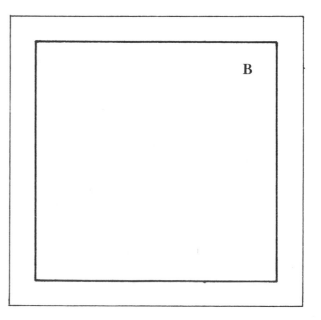

Measurements given <u>without</u> seam allowance

A — template given
B — template given
C — cut 17 squares 5 inches square
D — width of inner border—2 inches
E — width of outer border—8 inches

Make 18 pieced blocks

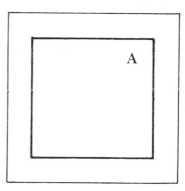

Assembly instructions:

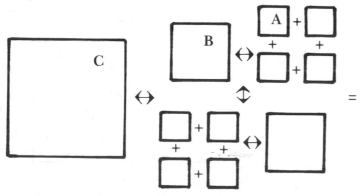

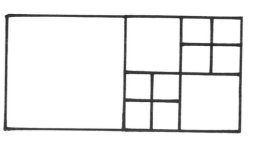

See Border Application Diagram, pg. 15.

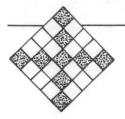

Irish Chain
Approximate size 47 x 55

Variation 1—Double Irish Chain

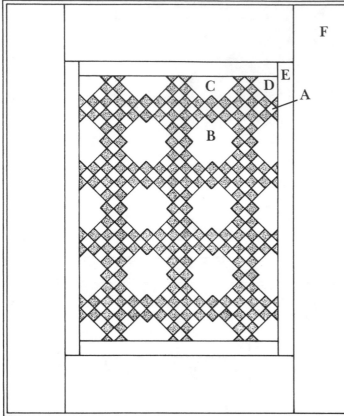

F

C   D   E

A

B

Measurements given <u>without</u> seam allowance

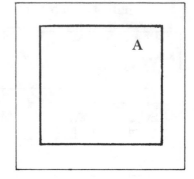

A

A — template given
B — cut 6-6¼ inch squares
C — cut 10 triangle

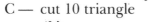

6¼ inches
6¼ inches

D — cut 4 triangles

4⅜ inches
4⅜ inches

E — width of inner border 2 inches
F — width of outer border 8 inches

Make 12 pieced blocks
Plain blocks and triangles need template A and partial template A appliqued in the corners to complete the pattern.

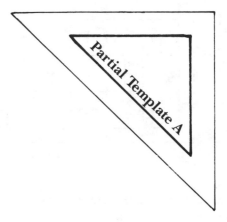

Partial Template A

Assembly instructions:

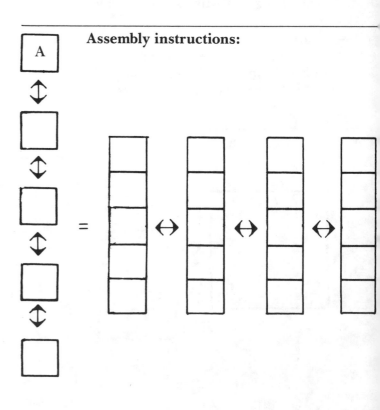

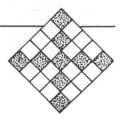

Variation 2—Single Irish Chain

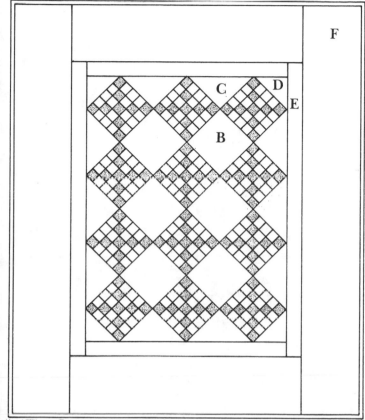

Proceed as in Variation 1 but eliminate appliqued squares on plain alternate blocks.

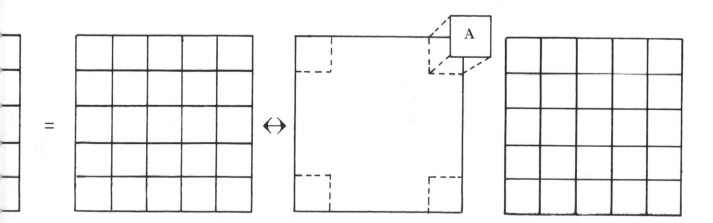

See Diagram 6, pg. 14 (Total Quilts Assembly).
See Border Application Diagram, pg. 15.

Log Cabin
Approximate size 45 x 53

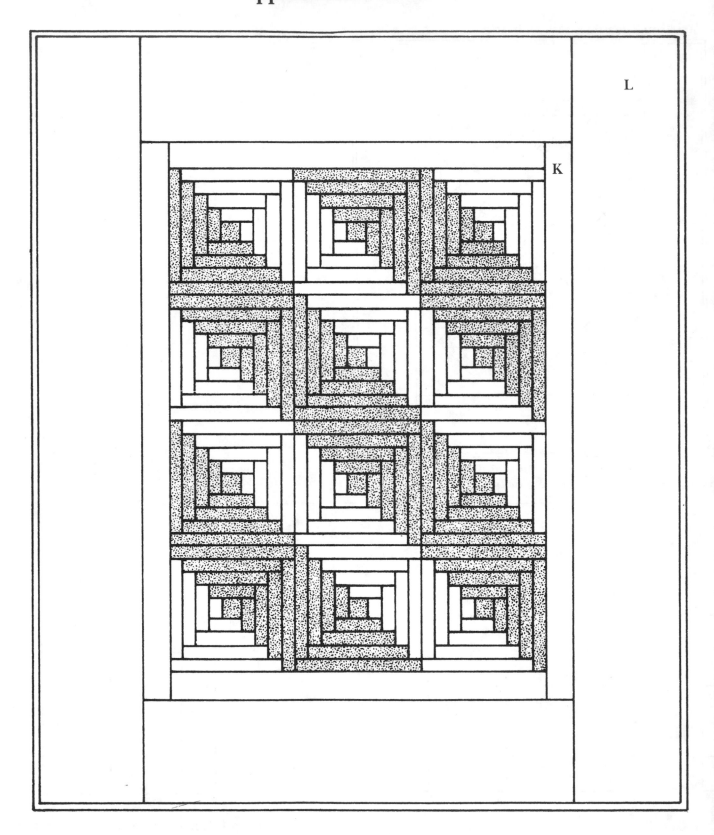

Assembly instructions:

K—width of inner border 2 inches
L—width of outer border 8 inches

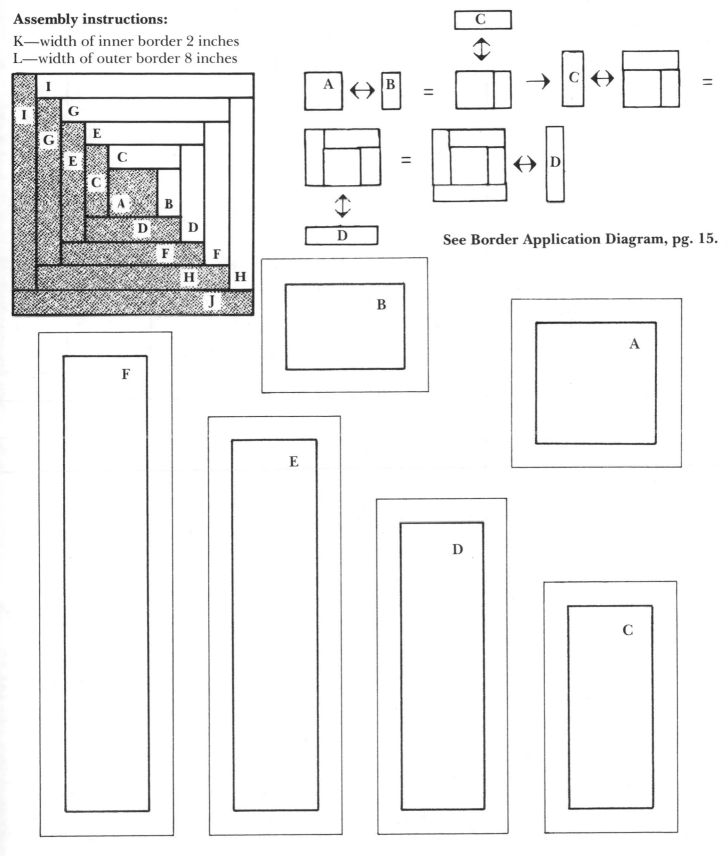

See Border Application Diagram, pg. 15.

G

H

I

J

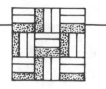

Rail Fence
Approximate size 47 x 56

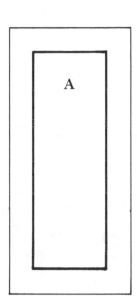

Measurements given <u>without</u> seam allowance

A — template given
B — width of inner border 2 inches
C — width of outer border 8 inches

Make 192 pieced blocks. Arrange in alternate
directions to each other.

Assembly instructions:

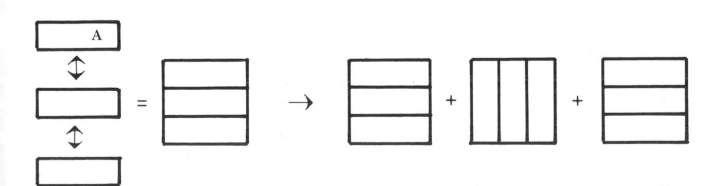

See Border Application Diagram, pg. 15.

Double T
Approximate size 46 x 58

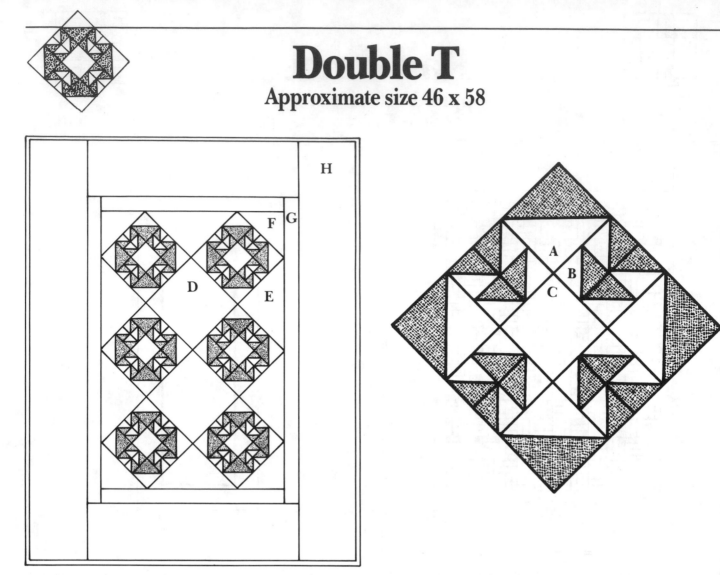

Measurements given <u>without</u> seam allowance

A — template given
B — template given
C — template given
D — cut 2-9 inch squares
E — cut 6 triangles

F — cut 4 triangles

G — width of inner border 2 inches
H — width of outer border 8 inches
Make 6 pieced blocks

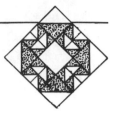

Assembly instructions:

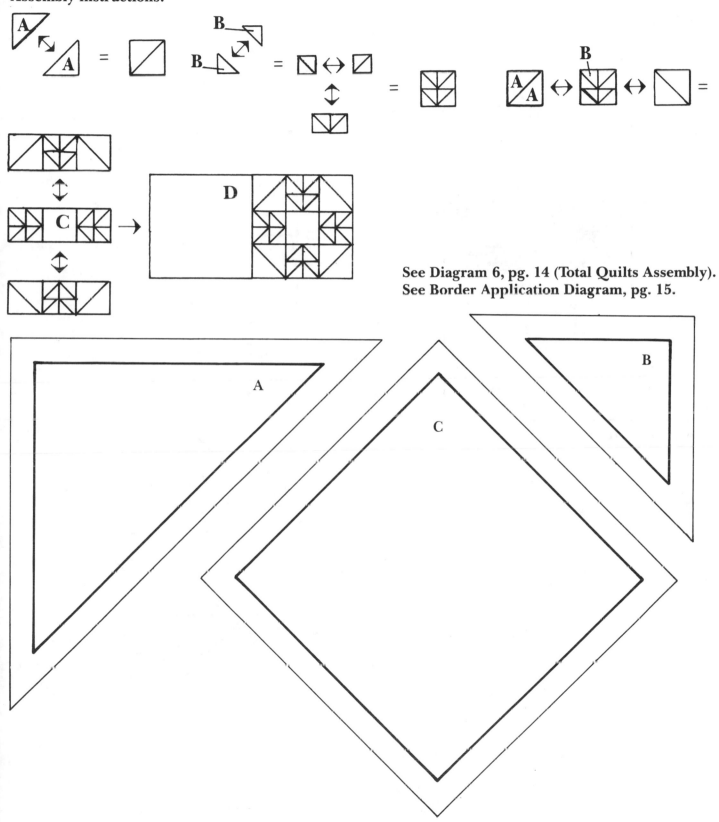

See Diagram 6, pg. 14 (Total Quilts Assembly).
See Border Application Diagram, pg. 15.

Stars
Approximate size 48 x 57

Variation 1—Lone Star

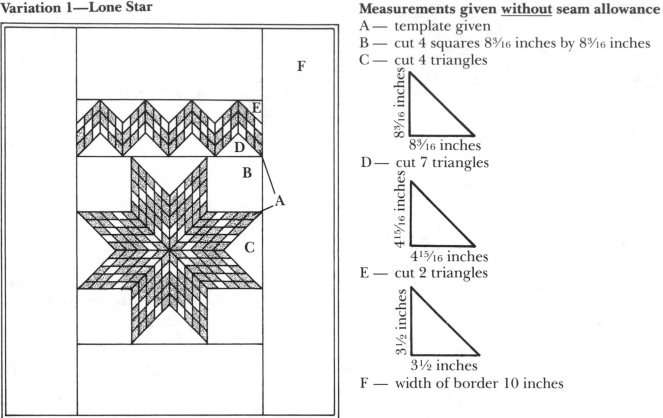

Measurements given <u>without</u> seam allowance

A — template given

B — cut 4 squares 8³⁄₁₆ inches by 8³⁄₁₆ inches

C — cut 4 triangles

8³⁄₁₆ inches / 8³⁄₁₆ inches

D — cut 7 triangles

4¹⁵⁄₁₆ inches / 4¹⁵⁄₁₆ inches

E — cut 2 triangles

3½ inches / 3½ inches

F — width of border 10 inches

Assembly instructions:

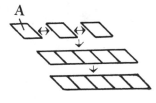

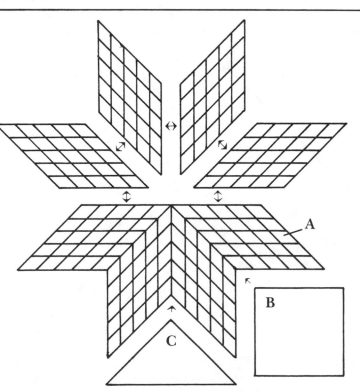

See Border Application Diagram, pg. 15.

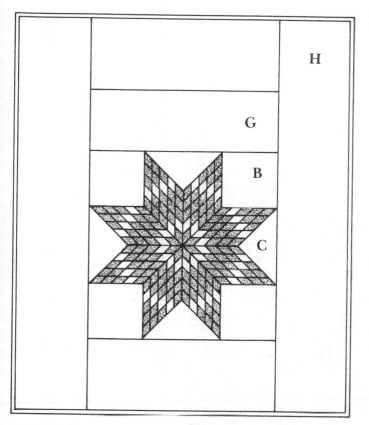

Variation 2—Lone star with plain pillow throw same as Variation 1 except eliminate D and E and replace with G-8½ x width of pieced star

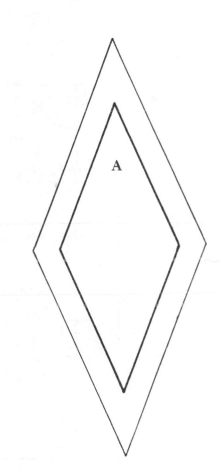

Jacob's Ladder
Approximate size 44 x 58

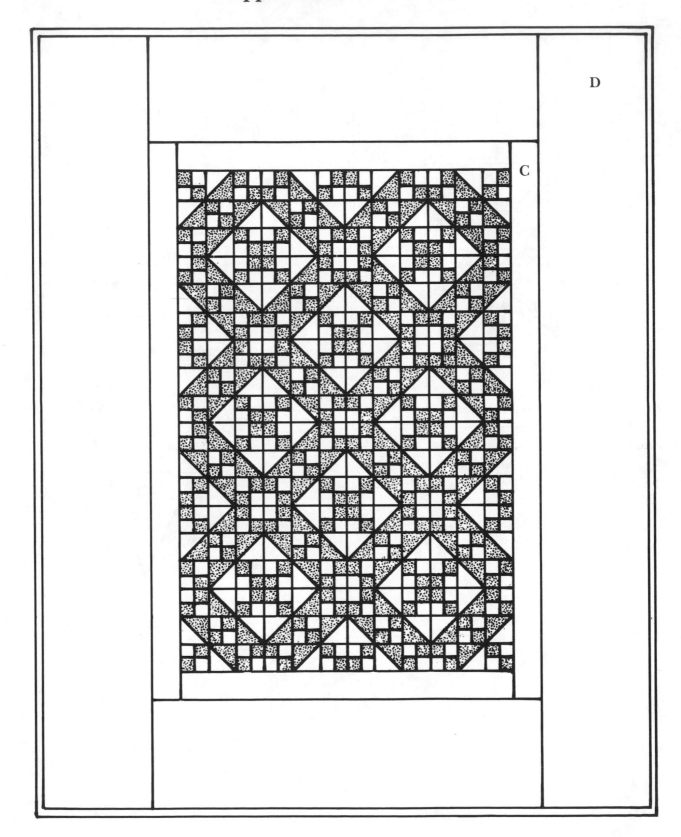

Measurements given <u>without</u> seam allowance

A — template given
B — template given
C — width of inner border 2 inches
D — width of outer border 8 inches

Make 24 pieced blocks

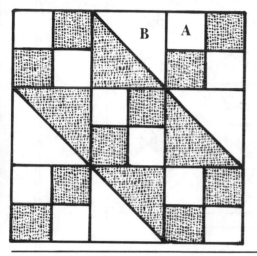

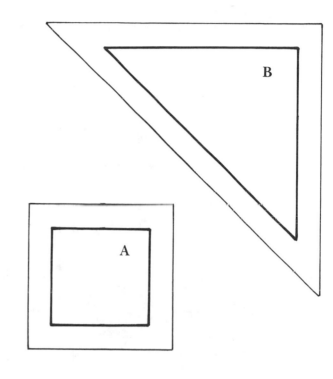

Assembly instructions:

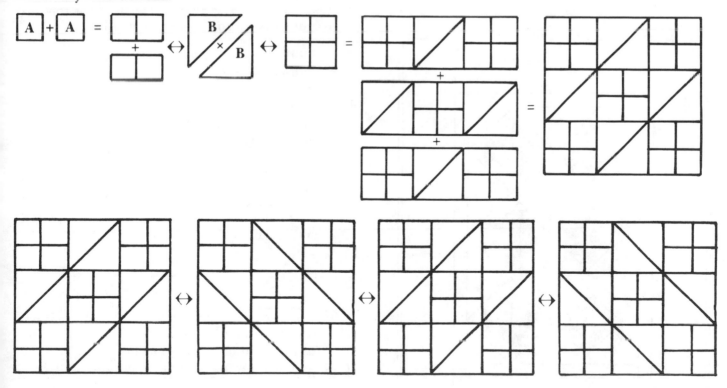

See Diagram 5, pg. 14 (Total Quilts Assembly).
See Border Application Diagram, pg. 15.

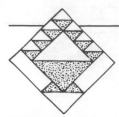

Baskets
Approximate size 46 x 58

Variation 1

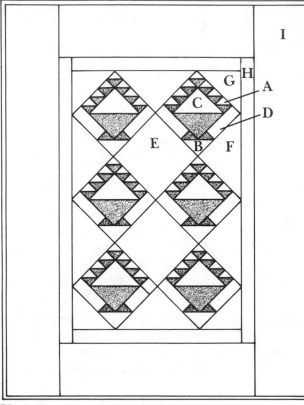

Variation 3

Variation 2

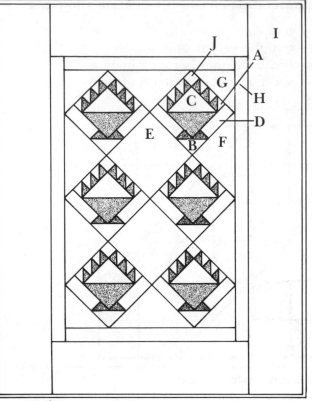

Measurements given <u>without</u> seam allowance

A — template given
B — template given
C — template given
D — template given
E — cut 2–9 inch squares
F — cut 6 triangles

9 inches / 9 inches triangle

G — cut 4 triangles

6⅜ inches / 6⅜ inches triangle

H — width of inner border 2 inches
I — width of outer border 8 inches
J — template given (used in variations 2 and 3)

Assembly instructions:

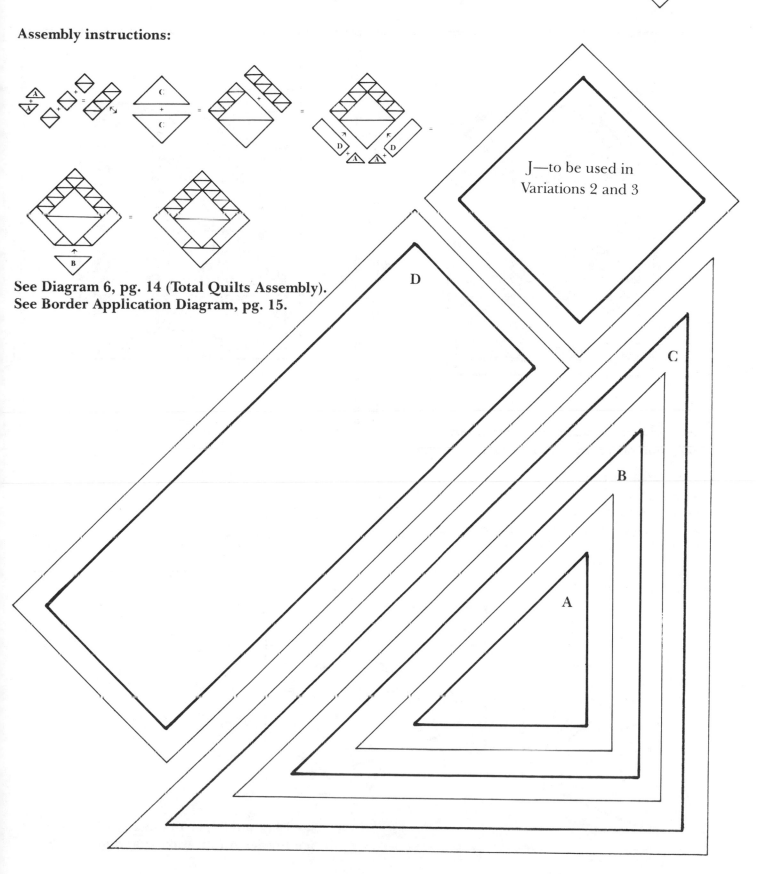

See Diagram 6, pg. 14 (Total Quilts Assembly).
See Border Application Diagram, pg. 15.

J—to be used in Variations 2 and 3

D

C

B

A

Fan
Approximate size 47 x 56

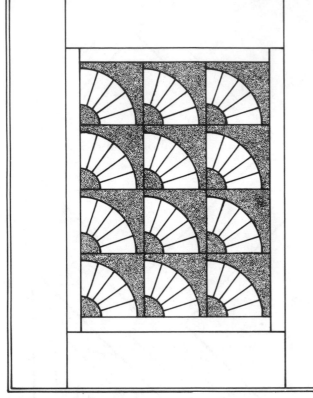

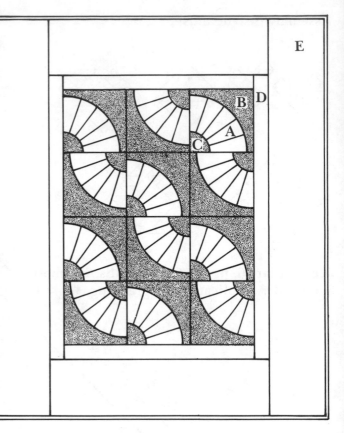

Measurements given <u>without</u> seam allowance

A — template given
B — template given
C — template given
D — width of inner border 2 inches
E — width of outer border 8 inches
Make 12 pieced blocks

Assembly instructions:

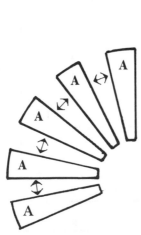

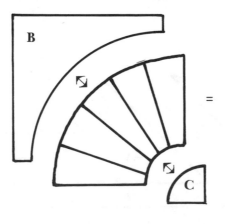

See Diagram 5, pg. 14 (Total Quilts Assembly).
See Border Application Diagram, pg. 15.

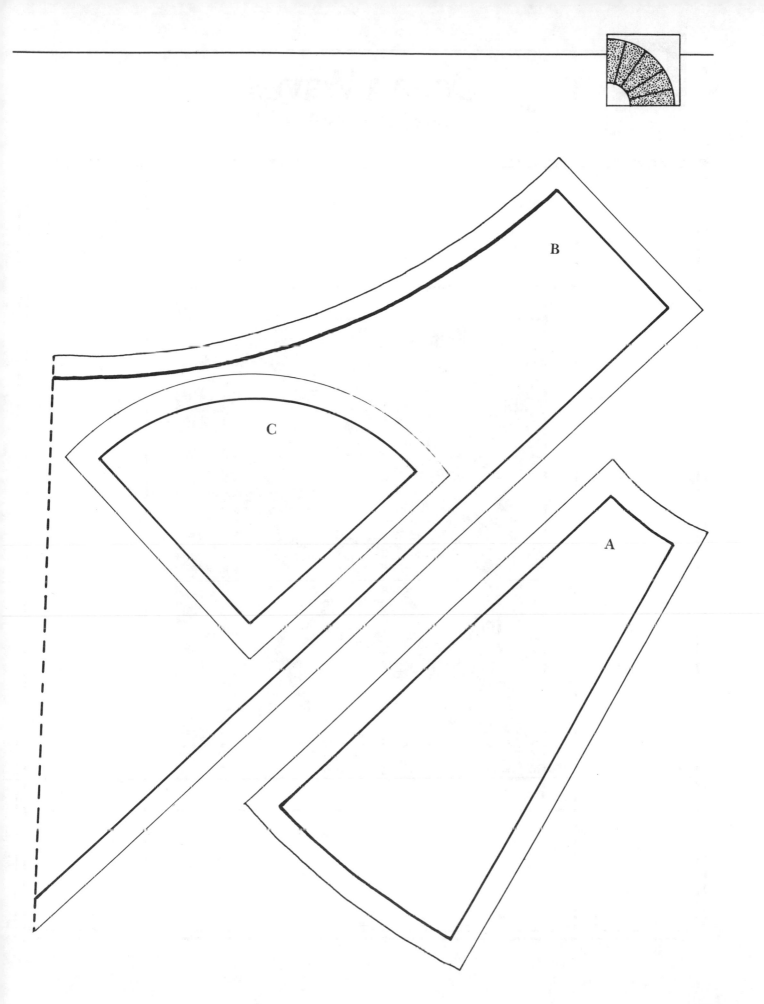

Ocean Waves
Approximate size 47 x 54

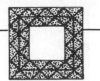

Measurements given <u>without</u> seam allowance

A — template given
B — template given
C — Cut 9 triangles

8½ inches / 8½ inches

D — Cut 2 triangles

6 inches / 6 inches

E — width of inner border 2 inches
F — width of outer border 8 inches

Make 15 pieced blocks   Make 11 half blocks

Make 2 quarter blocks

Assembly instructions:

A + A + A + A = ... = ...

See Border Application Diagram, pg. 15.

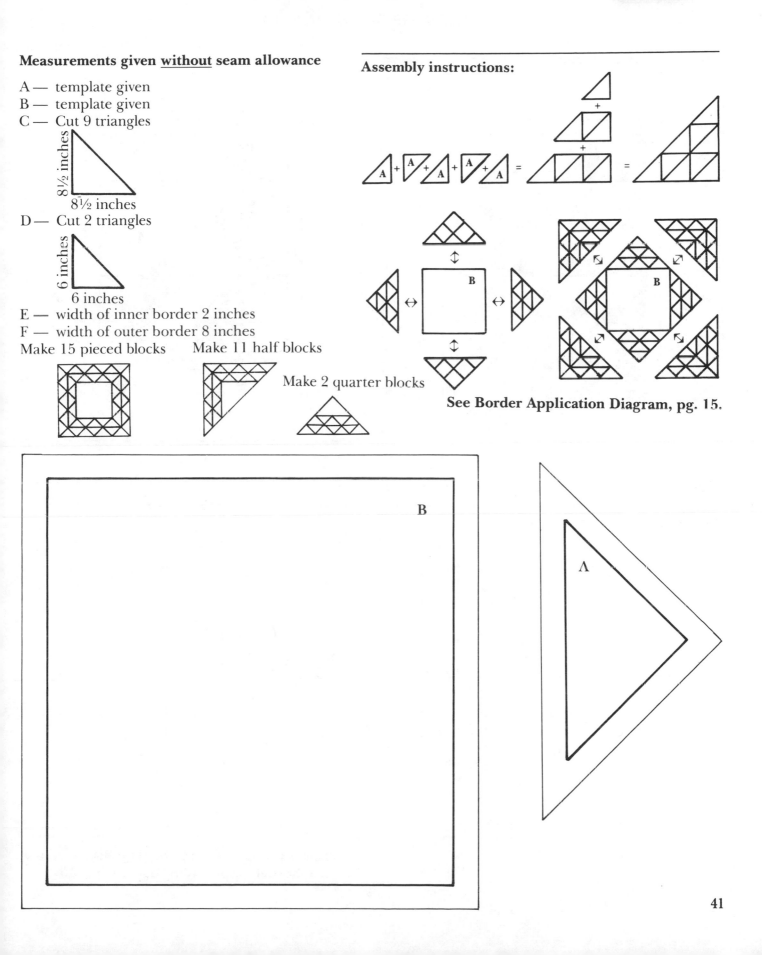

B

A

Roman Stripe
Approximate size 48 x 55

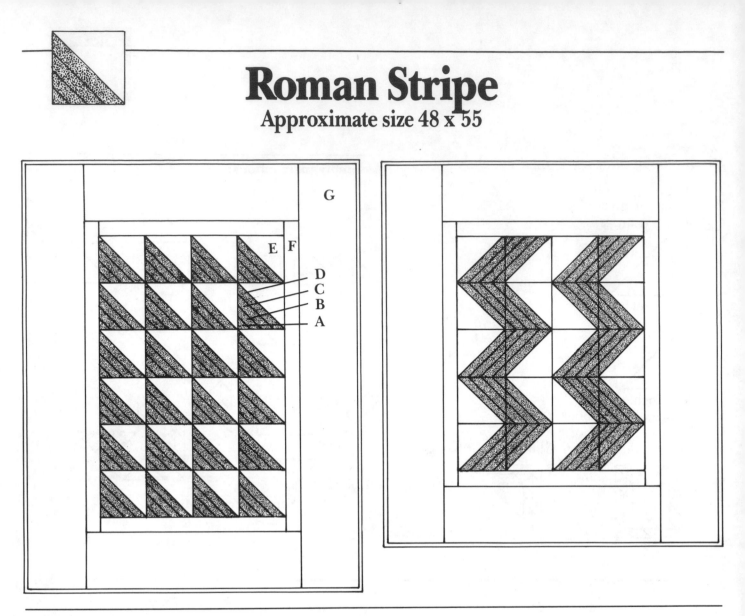

Assembly instructions:

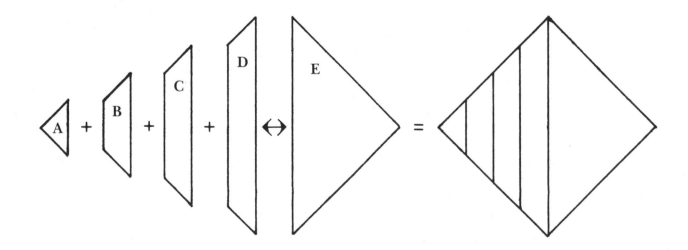

See Diagram 5, pg. 14 (Total Quilts Assembly).
See Border Application Diagram, pg. 15.

Measurements given <u>without</u> seam allowance

A — template given
B — template given
C — template given
D — template given
E — cut 24 triangles

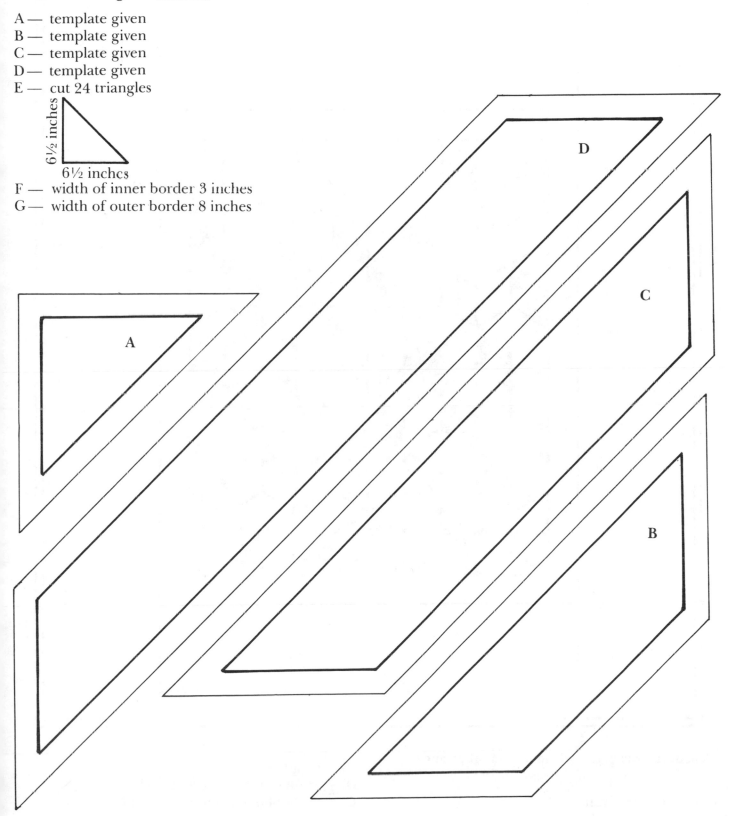

6½ inches
6½ inches

F — width of inner border 3 inches
G — width of outer border 8 inches

A

D

C

B

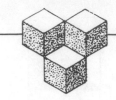

Tumbling Blocks
Approximate size 48 x 54

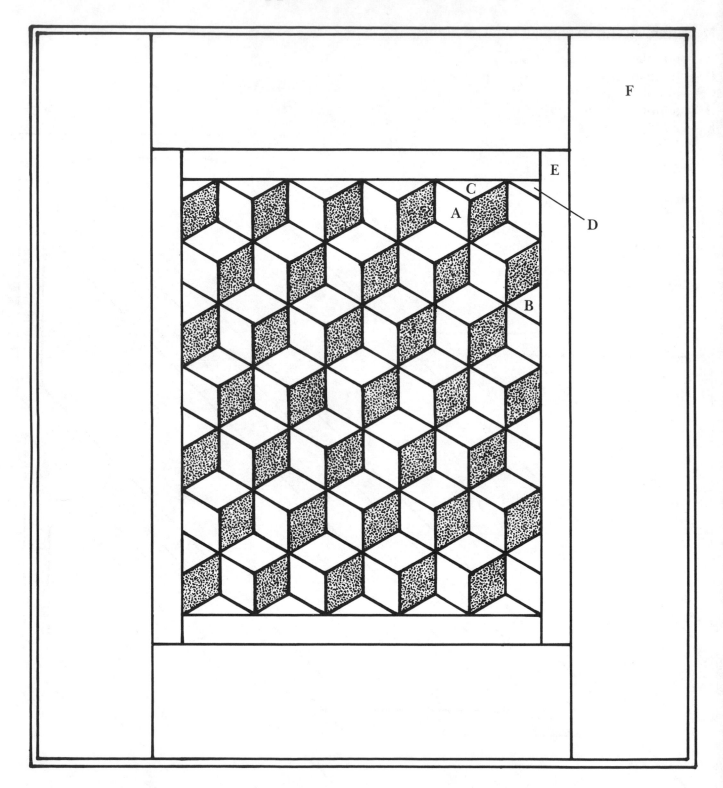

Measurements given <u>without</u> seam allowance

A — template given
B — template given

C — template given
D — width of inner border 2 inches
E — width of outer border 8 inches

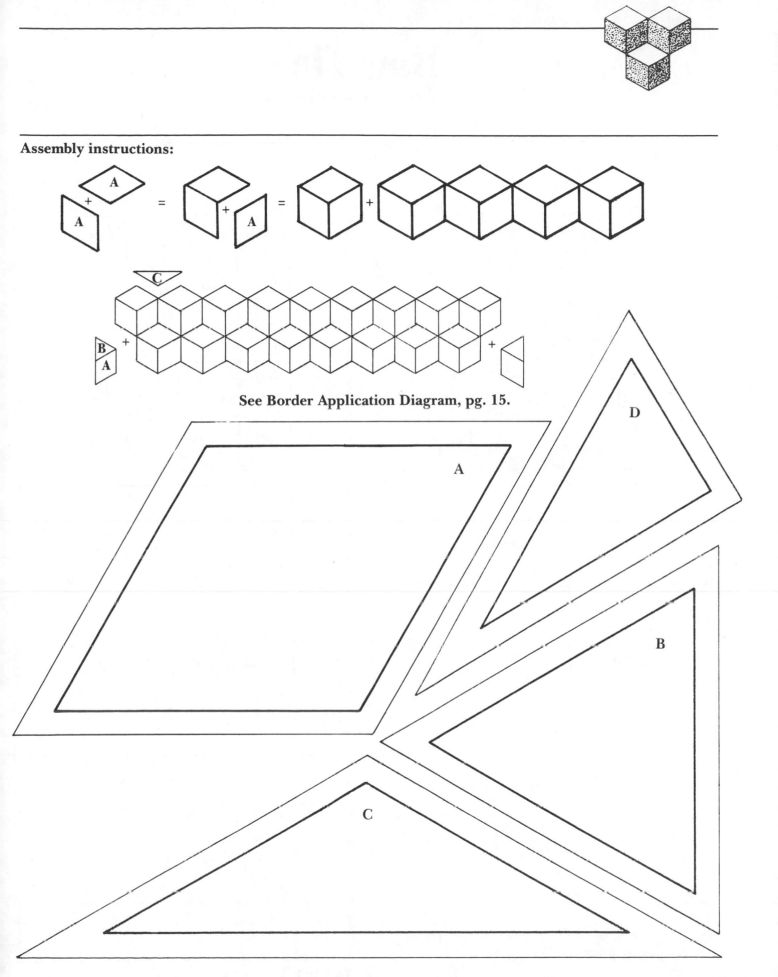

Assembly instructions:

See Border Application Diagram, pg. 15.

A

D

B

C

Bow Tie
Approximate size 45 x 55

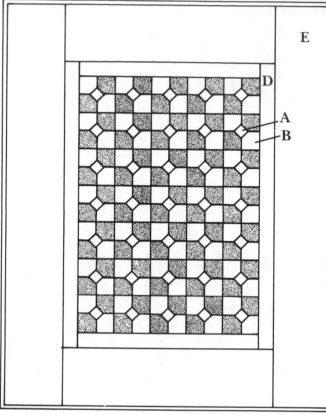

Variation 1

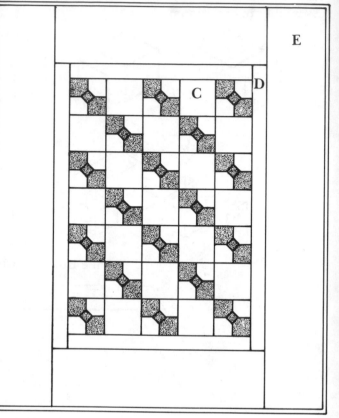

Variation 2

Measurements given <u>without</u> seam allowance

A — template given
B — template given
C — template given (used only for variations 2 and 3)
D — width of inner border 2 inches
E — width of outer border 8 inches
Make 35 pieced blocks (variation 2 make 12 pieced blocks)

Assembly instructions:

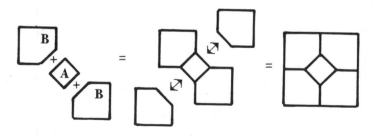

See Diagram 5, pg. 14 (Total Quilts Assembly).
See Border Application Diagram, pg. 15.

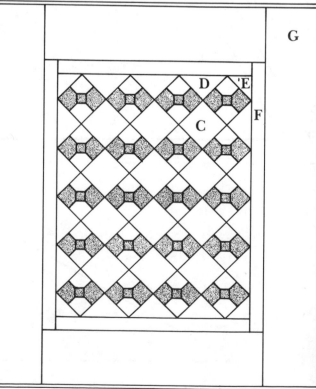

Variation 3

46

Variation 3
Measurements given <u>without</u> seam allowance

A — template given
B — template given
C — cut 12 squares template given
D — cut 14 triangles

5 inches (vertical) / 5 inches (horizontal)

E — cut 4 triangles

3½ inches (vertical) / 3½ inches (horizontal)

F — width of inner border 2 inches
G — width of outer border 8 inches
Make 20 pieced blocks

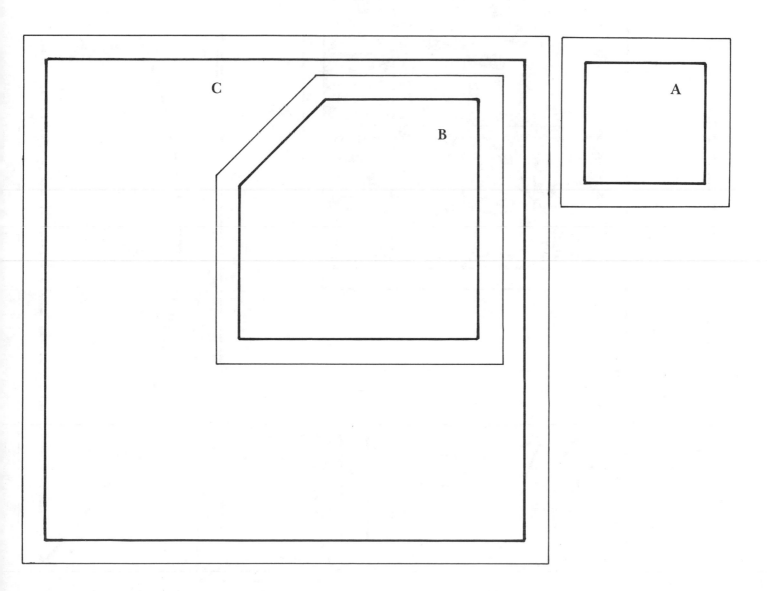

C

B

A

Robbing Peter to Pay Paul
Approximate size 48 x 55

Assembly instructions:

See Diagram 5, pg. 14 (Total Quilts Assembly).
See Border Application Diagram, pg. 15.

Measurements given <u>without</u> seam allowance

A— template given
B— template given
C— width of inner border 2 inches
D— width of outer border 8 inches
Make 20 pieced blocks

B

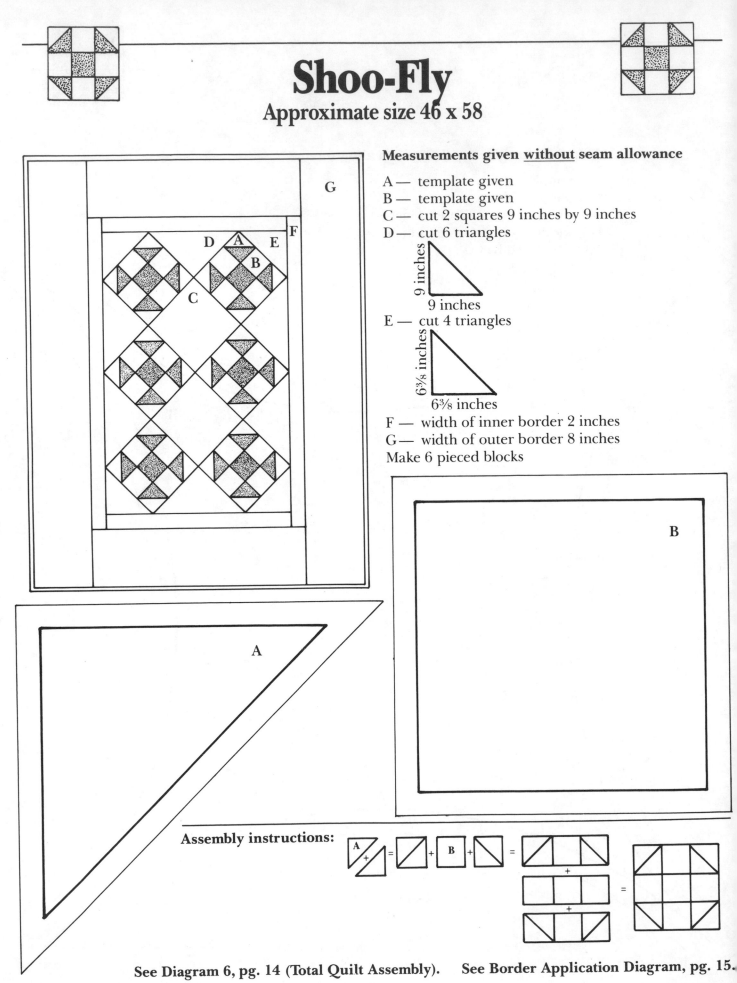

Shoo-Fly
Approximate size 46 x 58

Measurements given <u>without</u> seam allowance

A — template given
B — template given
C — cut 2 squares 9 inches by 9 inches
D — cut 6 triangles

9 inches / 9 inches

E — cut 4 triangles

6⅜ inches / 6⅜ inches

F — width of inner border 2 inches
G — width of outer border 8 inches
Make 6 pieced blocks

Assembly instructions:

See Diagram 6, pg. 14 (Total Quilt Assembly).   **See Border Application Diagram, pg. 15.**

Crown of Thorns
Approximate size 46 x 58

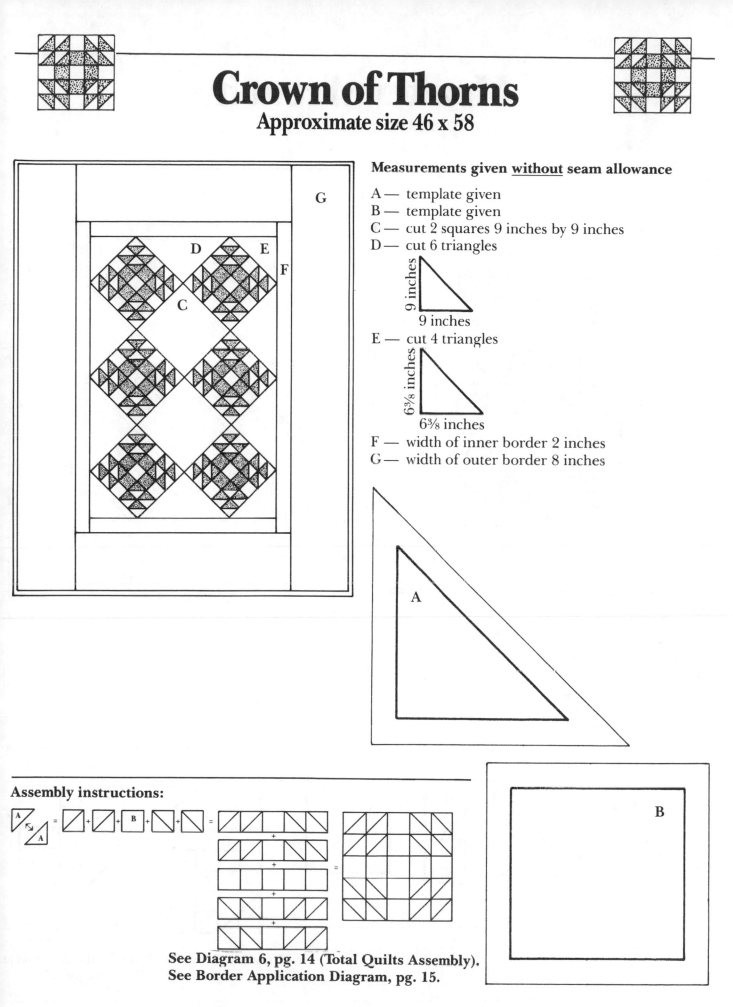

Measurements given <u>without</u> seam allowance

A — template given
B — template given
C — cut 2 squares 9 inches by 9 inches
D — cut 6 triangles

9 inches | 9 inches

E — cut 4 triangles

$6\frac{3}{8}$ inches | $6\frac{3}{8}$ inches

F — width of inner border 2 inches
G — width of outer border 8 inches

Assembly instructions:

See Diagram 6, pg. 14 (Total Quilts Assembly).
See Border Application Diagram, pg. 15.

Monkey Wrench
Approximate size 46 x 57

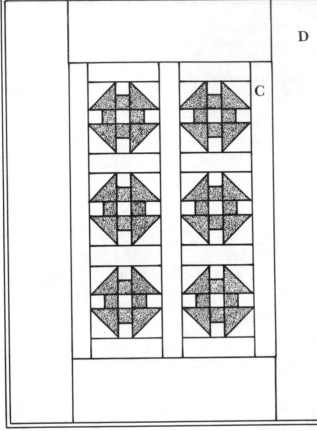

Variation 1

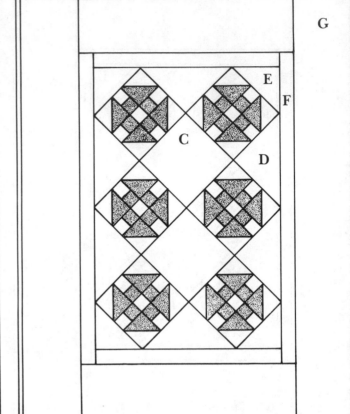

Variation 2

Measurements given <u>without</u> seam allowance

A— template given
B— template given
C— width of sashing and inner border 2½ inches
D— width of border 8 inches
Make 6 pieced blocks

Assembly instructions:

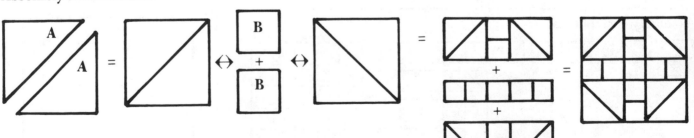

See Diagram 5, pg. 14 (Total Quilts Assembly)
See Border Application Diagram, pg. 15.

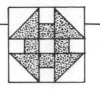

Variation 2
Approximate size 46x58
Measurements given <u>without</u> seam allowance
A— template given
B— template given
C— cut 2-9 inch squares
D— cut 6 triangles

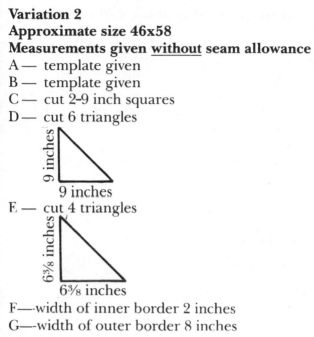

E.— cut 4 triangles

F—width of inner border 2 inches
G—width of outer border 8 inches
Make 6 pieced blocks

See Diagram 6, pg. 14 (Total Quilts Assembly).
See Border Application Diagram, pg. 15.

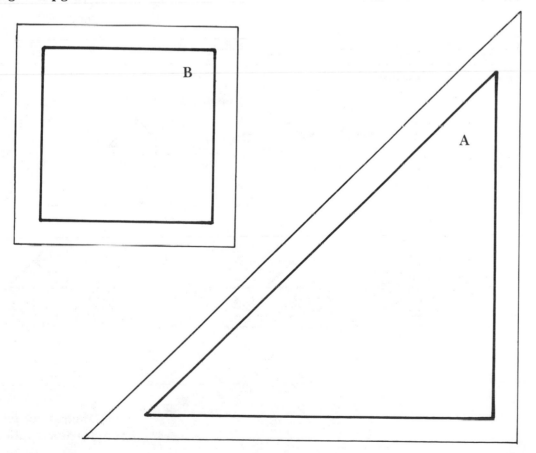

Carolina Lily
Approximate size 46 x 58

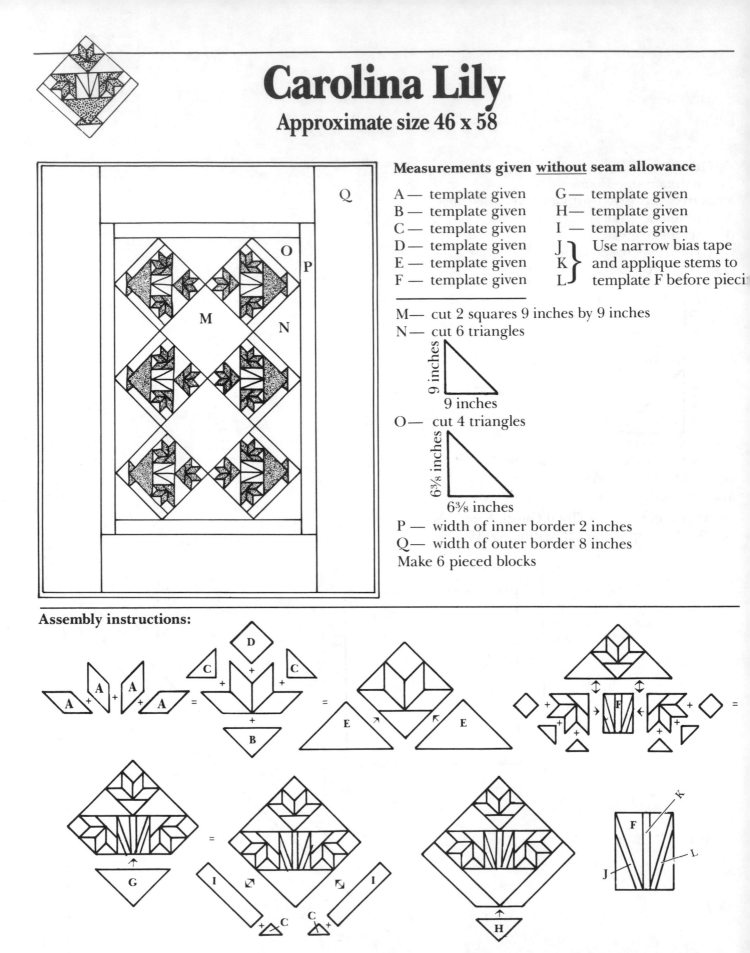

Measurements given <u>without</u> seam allowance

A — template given   G — template given
B — template given   H — template given
C — template given   I — template given
D — template given   J ⎫ Use narrow bias tape
E — template given   K ⎬ and applique stems to
F — template given   L ⎭ template F before pieci

M— cut 2 squares 9 inches by 9 inches
N— cut 6 triangles
O— cut 4 triangles
P — width of inner border 2 inches
Q — width of outer border 8 inches
Make 6 pieced blocks

Assembly instructions:

See Diagram 6, pg. 14 (Total Quilts Assembly).
See Border Application Diagram, pg. 15.

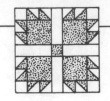

Bear Paw
Approximate size 46 x 58

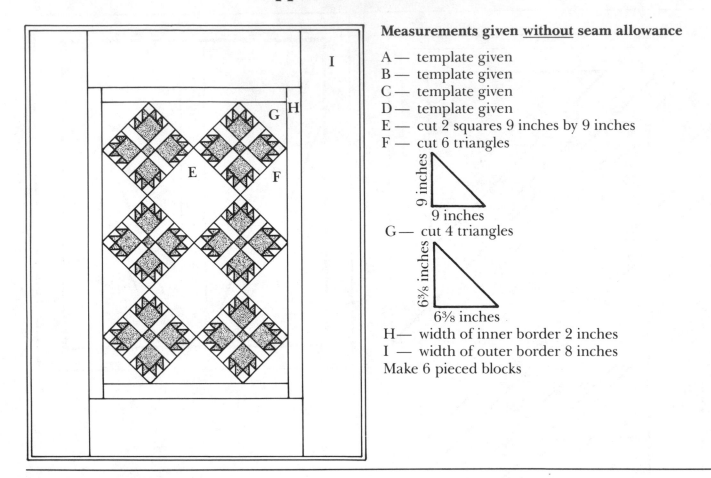

Measurements given <u>without</u> seam allowance

A — template given
B — template given
C — template given
D — template given
E — cut 2 squares 9 inches by 9 inches
F — cut 6 triangles

9 inches / 9 inches

G — cut 4 triangles

6⅜ inches / 6⅜ inches

H — width of inner border 2 inches
I — width of outer border 8 inches
Make 6 pieced blocks

Assembly instructions:

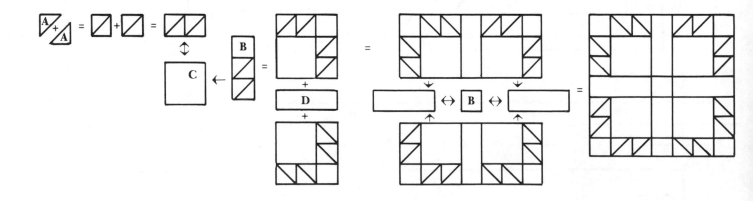

See Diagram 6, pg. 14 (Total Quilts Assembly).
See Border Application Diagram, pg. 15.

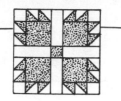

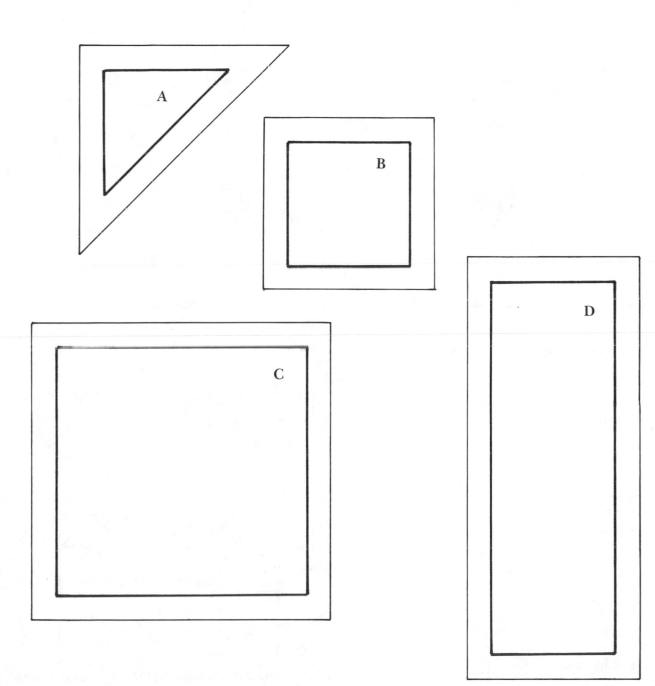

A

B

C

D

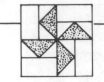

Pinwheel
Approximate size 46 x 58

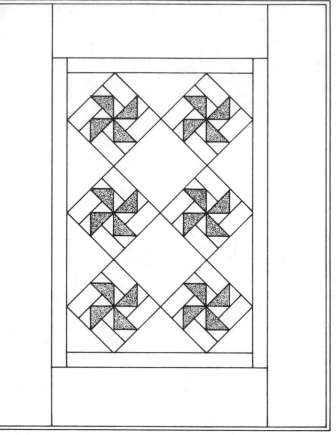

Variation 1

Variation 2

Measurements given <u>without</u> seam allowance
A — template given
B — template given
C — template given (used in variation 2)
D — cut 2 squares 9 inches x 9 inches
E — cut 6 triangles

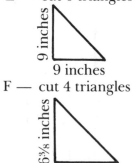

9 inches

9 inches

F — cut 4 triangles

6⅜ inches

6⅜ inches

G — width of inner border 2 inches
H — width of outer border 8 inches
Make 6 pieced blocks

Assembly instructions:

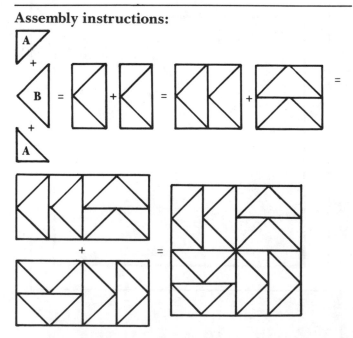

See Diagram 6, pg. 14 (Total Quilts Assembly).
See Border Application Diagram, pg. 15.

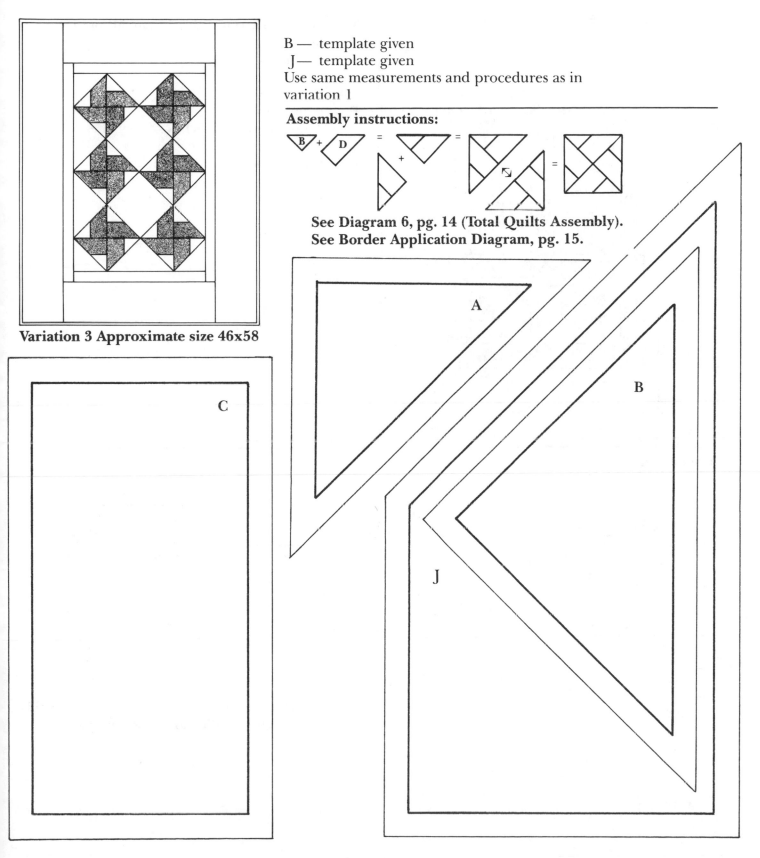

B — template given
J— template given
Use same measurements and procedures as in variation 1

Assembly instructions:

See Diagram 6, pg. 14 (Total Quilts Assembly).
See Border Application Diagram, pg. 15.

Variation 3 Approximate size 46x58

Garden Maze
Approximate size 48 x 60

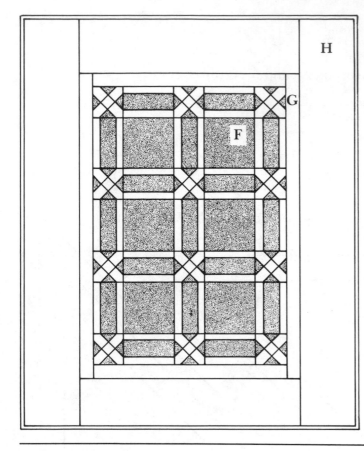

Measurements given <u>without</u> seam allowance

A — template given
B — template given
C — template given
D — template given
E — template given
F — cut 6 squares 7½ inches x 7½ inches
G — width of inner border 2 inches
H — width of outer border 8 inches

Assembly instructions:

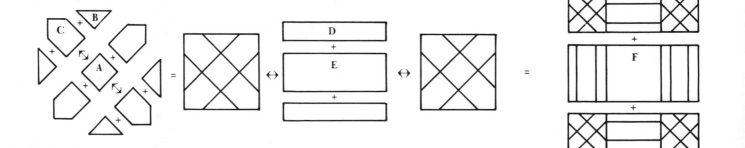

See Diagram 5, pg. 14 (Total Quilts Assembly).
See Border Application Diagram, pg. 15.

A

B

C

D

E

Railroad Crossing
Approximate size 48 × 62

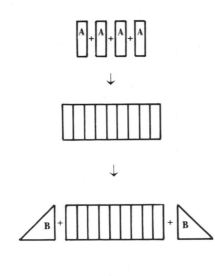

Measurements given <u>without</u> seam allowance
A—template given
B—template given
C—cut 8 squares 6¾ inches by 6¾ inches
D—template given
E—template given
F—template given
G—width of inner border 2 inches
H—width of outer border 8 inches

Assembly instructions:

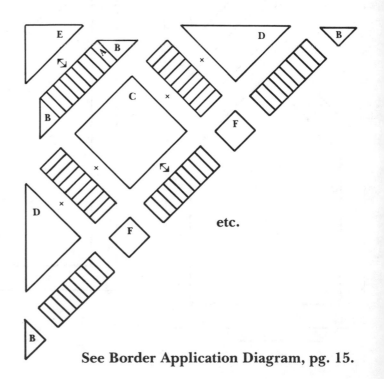

etc.

See Border Application Diagram, pg. 15.

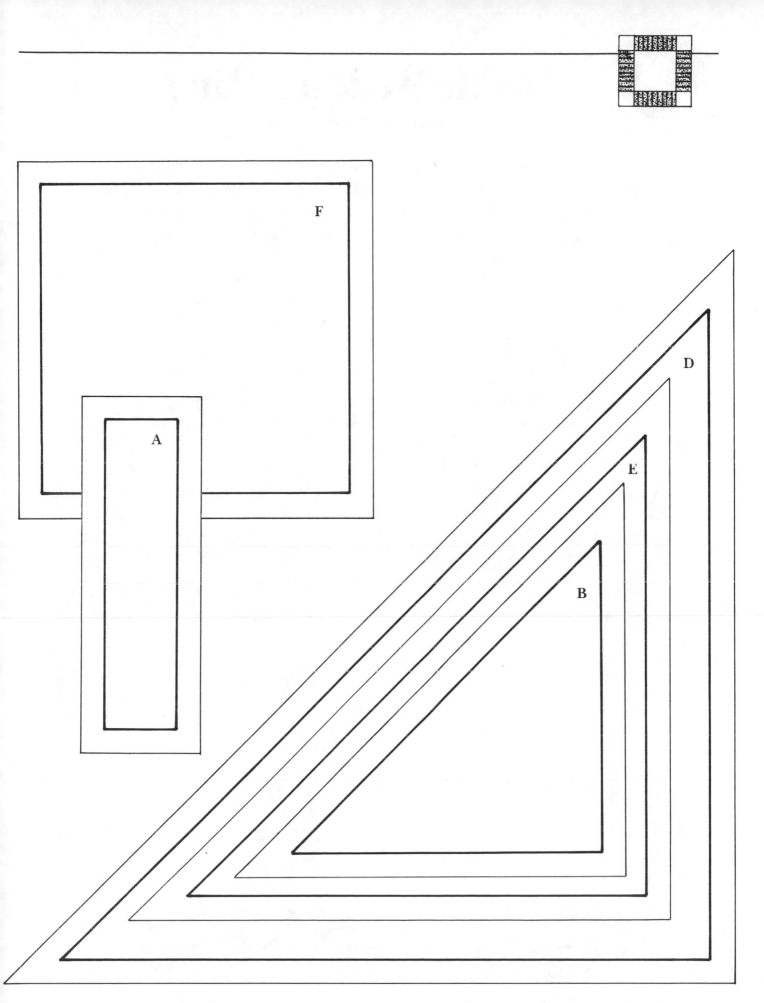

Double Wedding Ring

Approximate size 40 x 58

A — template given
B — template given
C — template given
D — template given
E — template given
F — template given

Assembly instructions:

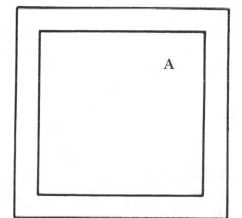

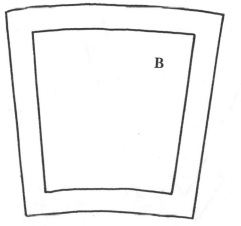

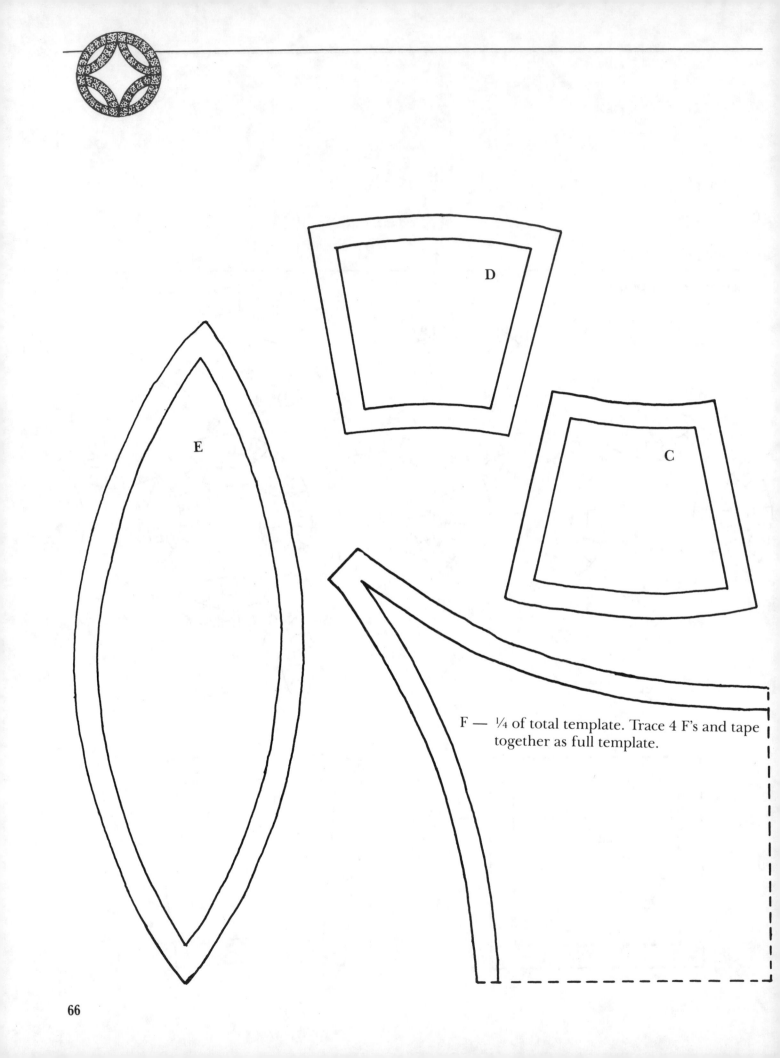

D

C

E

F — ¼ of total template. Trace 4 F's and tape together as full template.

Diagonal Triangles
Approximate size 44 x 52

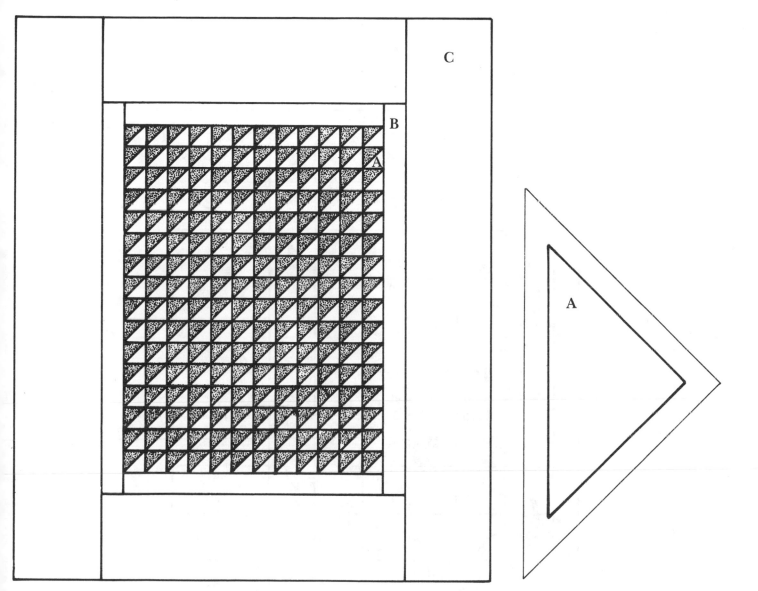

Measurements given <u>without</u> seam allowance

A— template given
B — width of inner border 2 inches
C — width of outer border 8 inches

Assembly instructions:

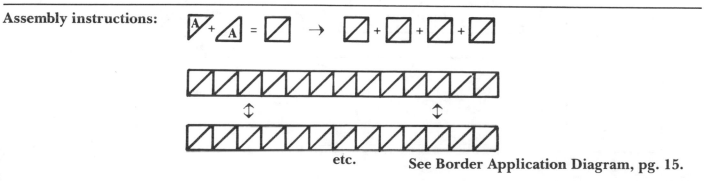

etc.   **See Border Application Diagram, pg. 15.**

Drunkard's Path
Approximate size 48 x 62

Measurements given <u>without</u> seam allowance

A — template given
B — template given
C — width of inner border 2 inches
D — width of outer border 8 inches
Make 96 pieced blocks. Alternate placement of
blocks to match diagram.

Assembly instructions:

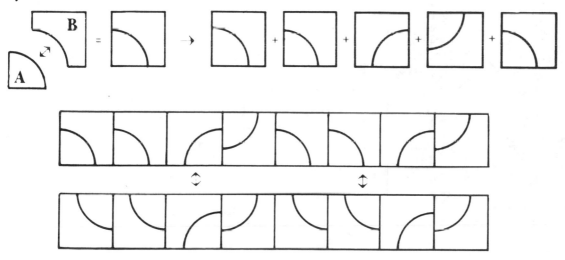

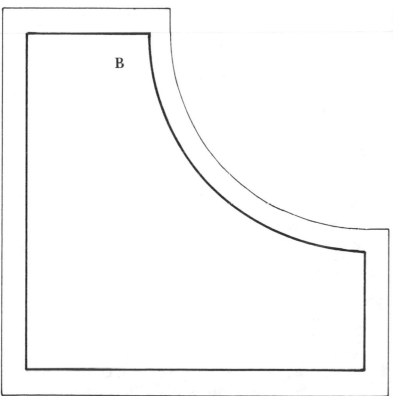

See Diagram 5, pg. 14 (Total Quilts Assembly).
See Border Application Diagram, pg. 15.

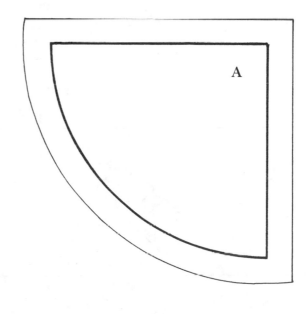

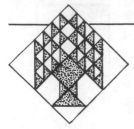

Tree of Life
Approximate size 46 x 58

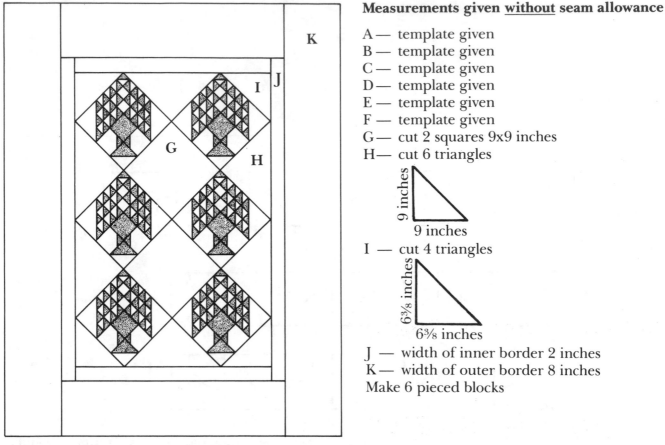

Measurements given <u>without</u> seam allowance

A — template given
B — template given
C — template given
D — template given
E — template given
F — template given
G — cut 2 squares 9x9 inches
H — cut 6 triangles

9 inches / 9 inches

I — cut 4 triangles

6⅜ inches / 6⅜ inches

J — width of inner border 2 inches
K — width of outer border 8 inches
Make 6 pieced blocks

Assembly instructions:

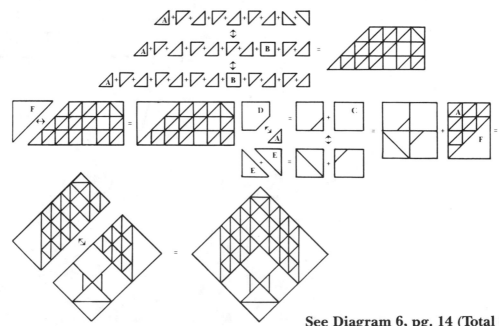

See Diagram 6, pg. 14 (Total Quilts Assembly).
See Border Application Diagram, pg. 15.

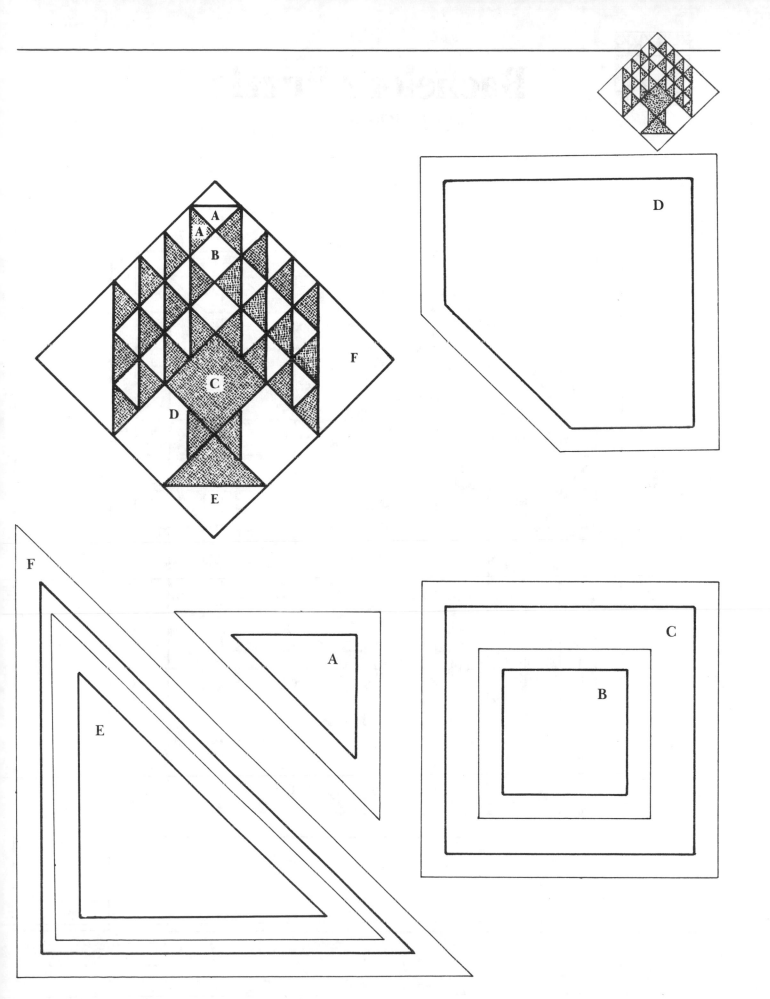

A

A

B

F

C

D

E

D

F

E

A

C

B

Bachelor's Puzzle
Approximate size 46 x 50

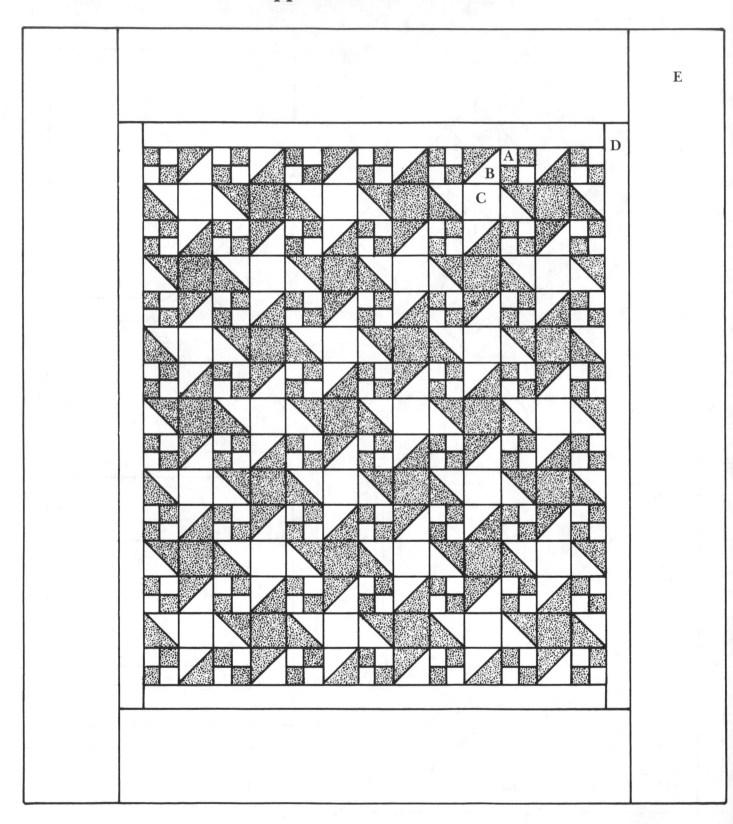

Measurements given <u>without</u> seam allowance

A — template given
B — template given
C — template given
D — width of inner border 2 inches
E — width of outer border 8 inches
Pieced blocks must be alternated as in diagram to
create the proper pattern

Assembly instructions:

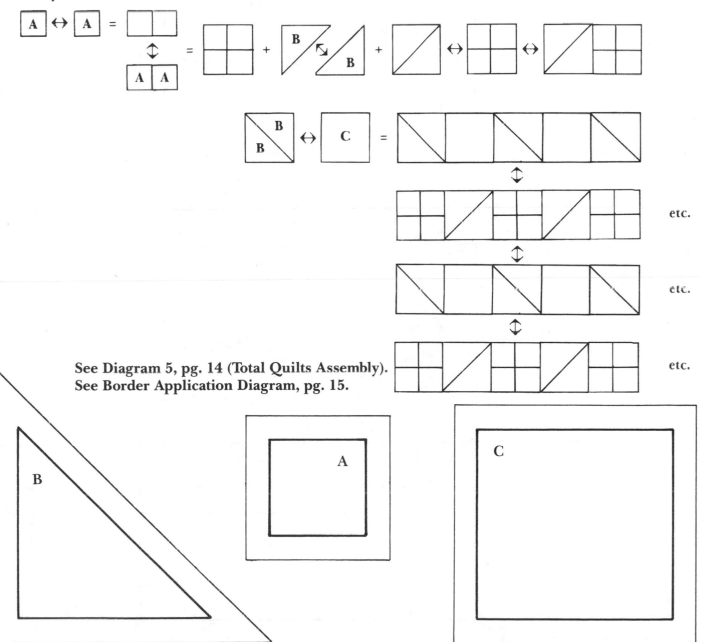

See Diagram 5, pg. 14 (Total Quilts Assembly).
See Border Application Diagram, pg. 15.

Rolling Stone
Approximate size 46 x 58

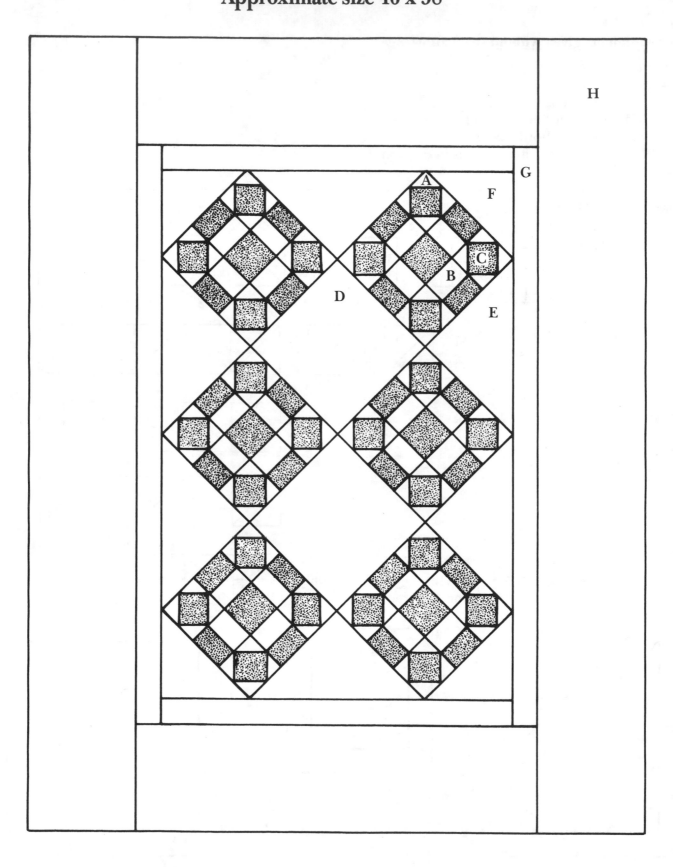

Measurements given <u>without</u> seam allowance

A — template given
B — template given
C — template given
D — cut 2 squares 9 by 9 inches
E — cut 6 triangles

9 inches (vertical)
9 inches (horizontal)

F — cut 4 triangles

6⅜ inches (vertical)
6⅜ inches (horizontal)

G — width of inner border 2 inches
H — width of outer border 8 inches
Make 6 pieced blocks

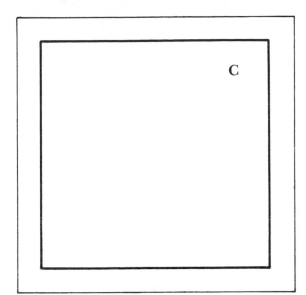

C

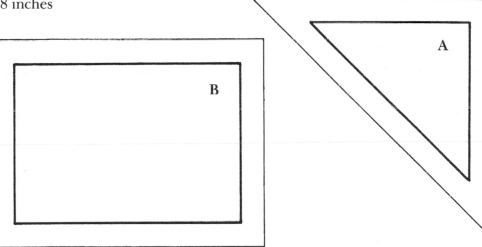

B

A

Assembly instructions:

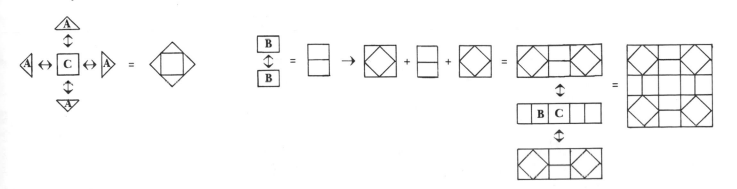

See Diagram 6, pg. 14 (Total Quilts Assembly).
See Border Application Diagram, pg. 15.

Quilting Templates

Following are several traditional quilting templates given in full size. Many of the templates extend over several pages. To use, pull out template section along perforation. Match corresponding letters along dotted lines and tape pages together to form the complete template.

One quarter of the Circular Feather is given. To make a complete circle, trace the section given, make a one-quarter turn, and trace again. Repeat until circle is complete.

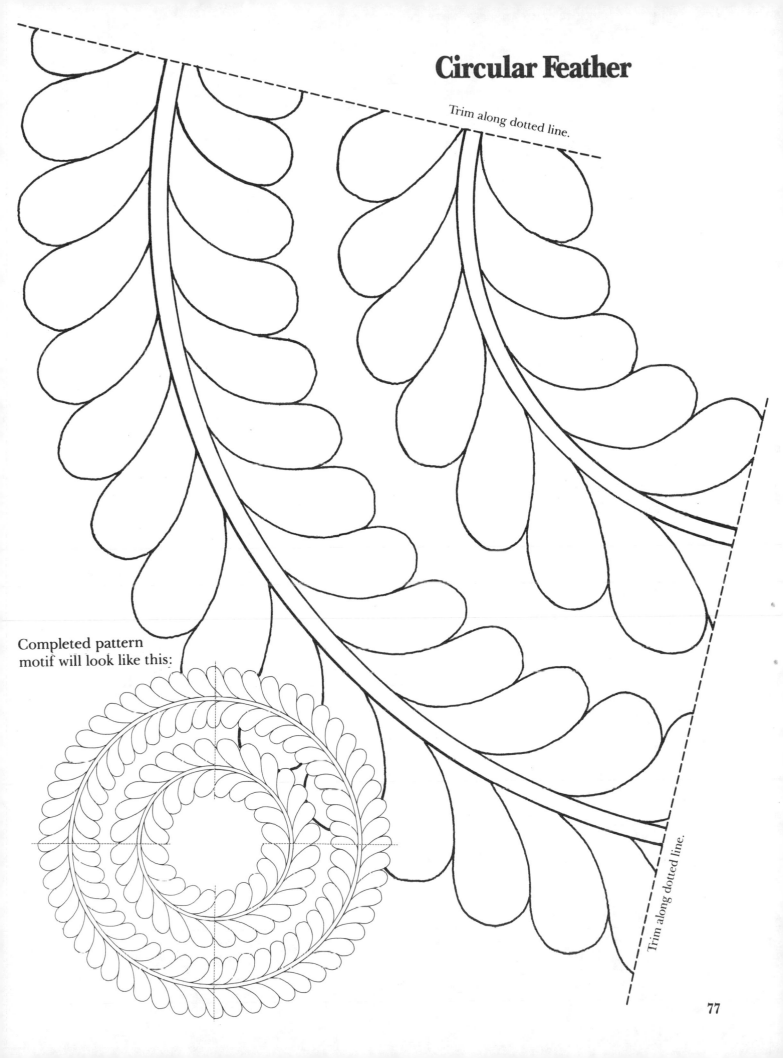

Circular Feather

Trim along dotted line.

Completed pattern
motif will look like this:

Trim along dotted line.

Triangular Rose—i.

Completed pattern motif will look like this:

To create finished template, match corresponding letters along dotted lines, and tape.

M

Trim along dotted line.

M

79

Triangular Rose—ii.

Trim along dotted line.

M   M

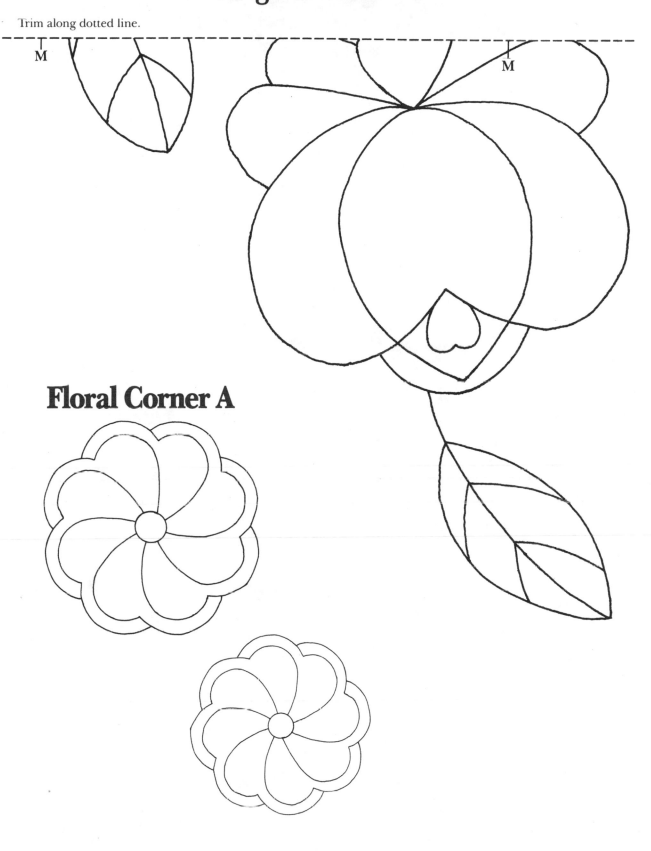

Floral Corner A

Feather Border—i.

Completed pattern motif will look like this:

To create finished template, match corresponding
letters along dotted lines, and tape.

D

Feather Border—ii.

D   D

E   E

Feather Border—iii.

Trim along dotted line.

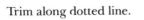

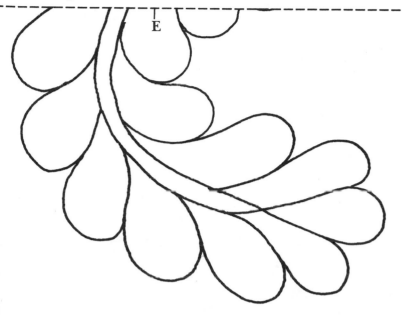

E

E

Ivy Leaf

Floral Corner B

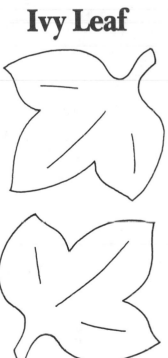

Fiddlehead Fern—i.

Completed pattern motif will look like this:

To create finished template, match corresponding letters along dotted lines, and tape.

Trim along dotted line.

F   F

Fiddlehead Fern—ii.

Floral Corner C

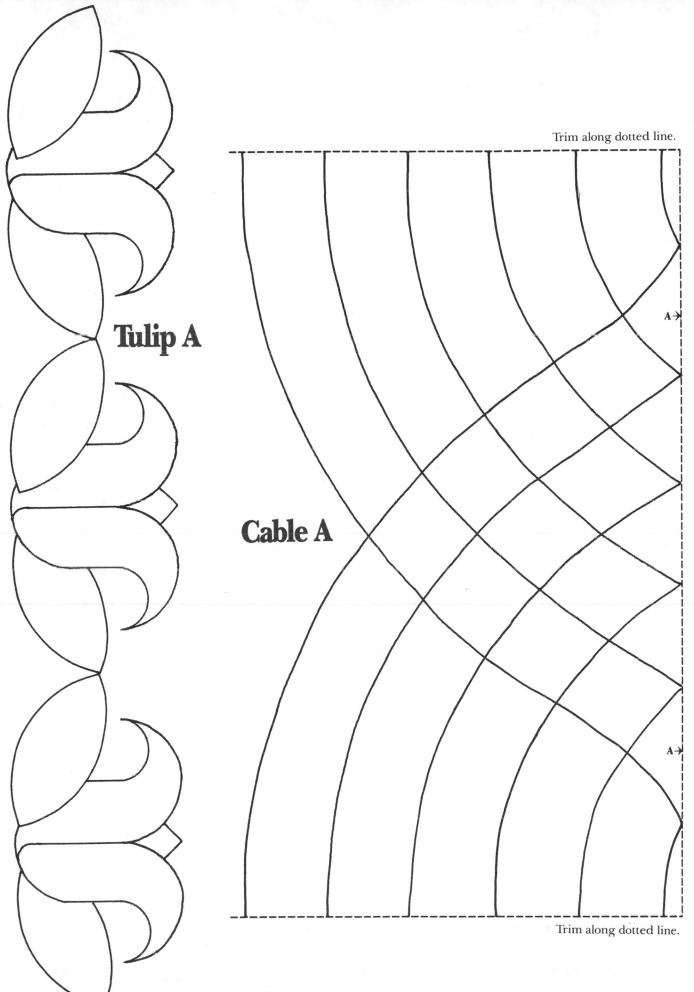

Tulip A

Cable A

Trim along dotted line.

A→

A→

A→

Trim along dotted line.

Trim along dotted line.

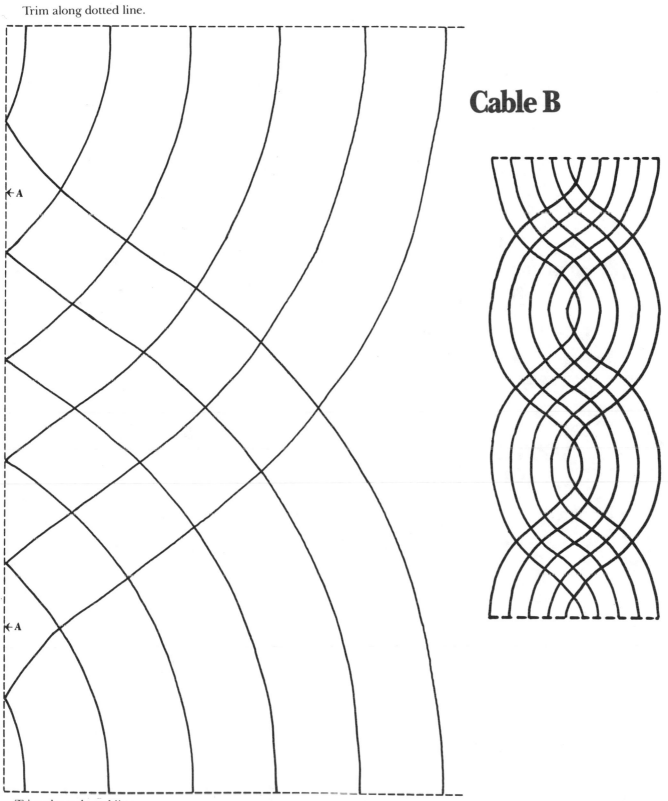

← A

← A

Cable B

Trim along dotted line.

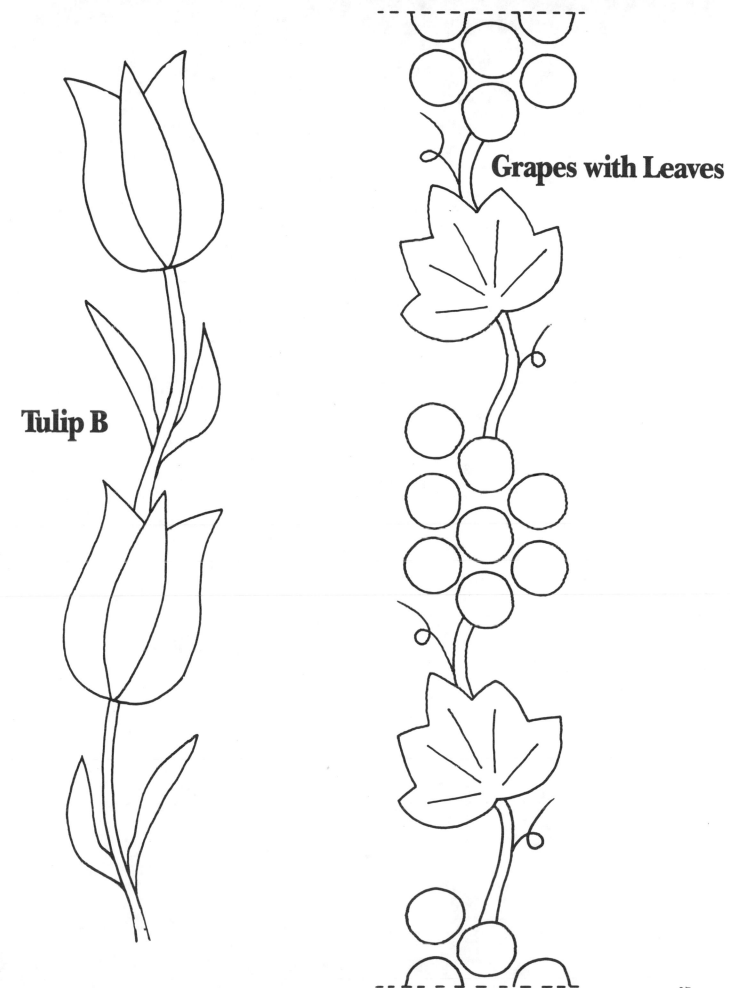

Tulip B

Grapes with Leaves

97

Pumpkin Seed

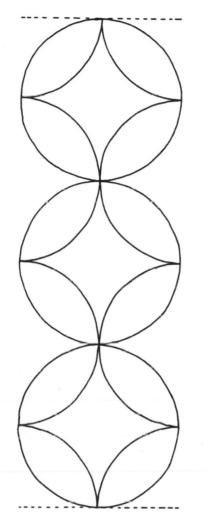

Floral Border Design

Dogwood

Fan A

Basket with Tulip—i.

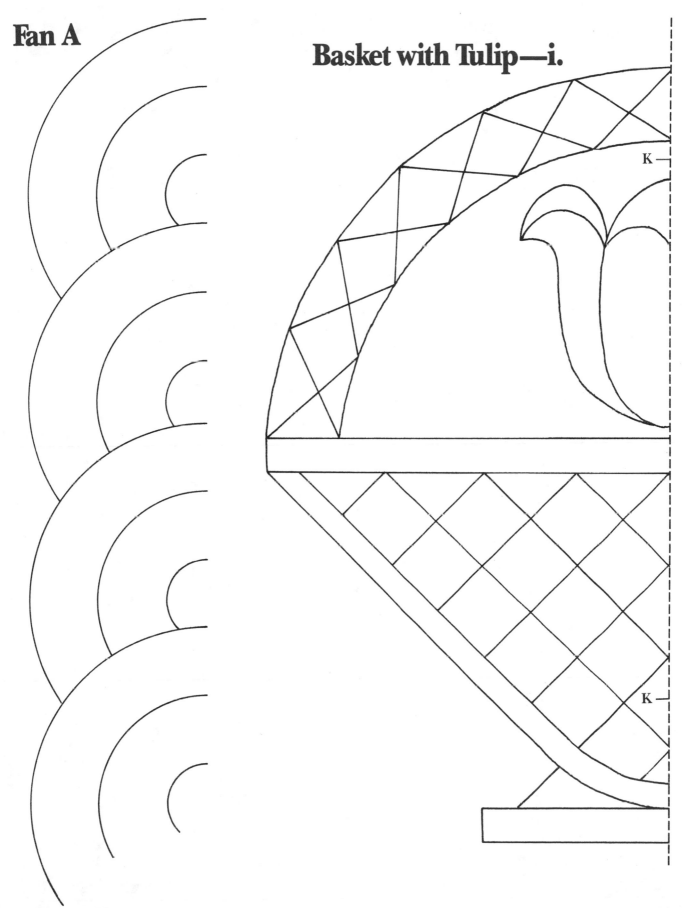

K

K

Basket with Tulip—ii.

K

K

Leaves

Trim along dotted line.

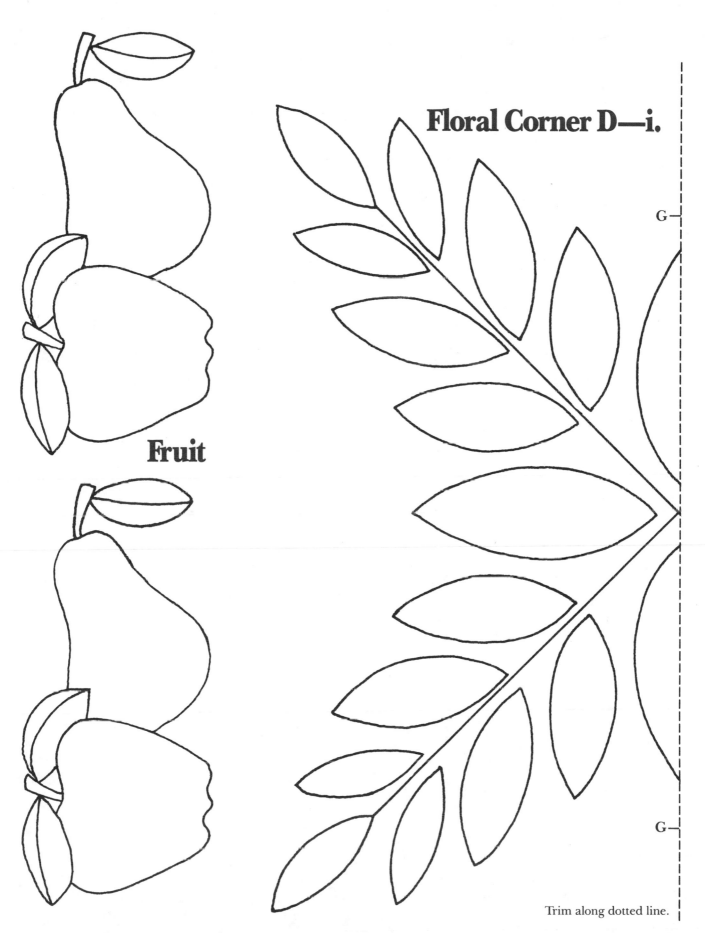

Floral Corner D—i.

Fruit

G—

G—

Trim along dotted line.

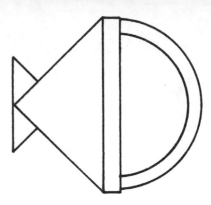

Floral Corner D—ii.

—G

—G

Trim along dotted line.

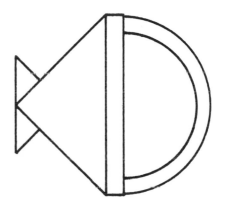

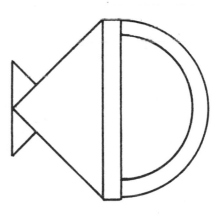

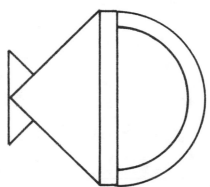

Feather Heart with Cross-Hatching

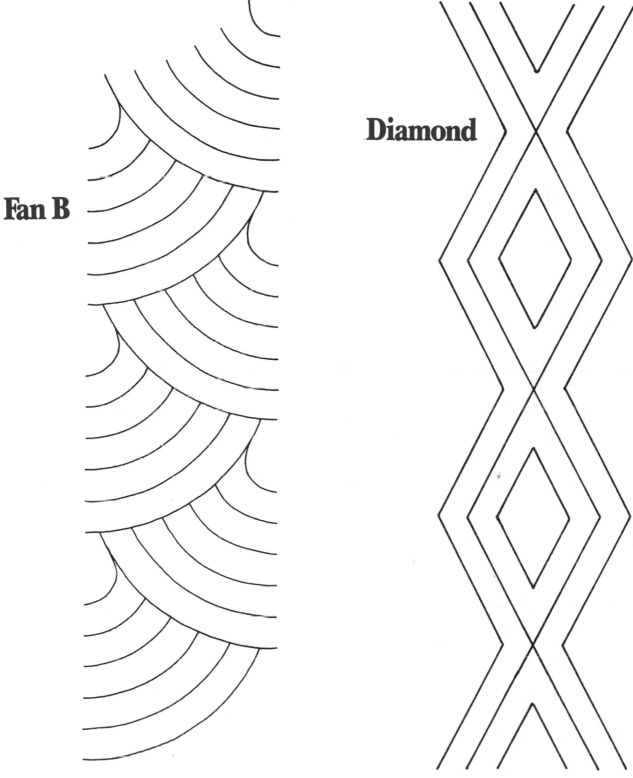

Fan B

Diamond

Floral Corner E

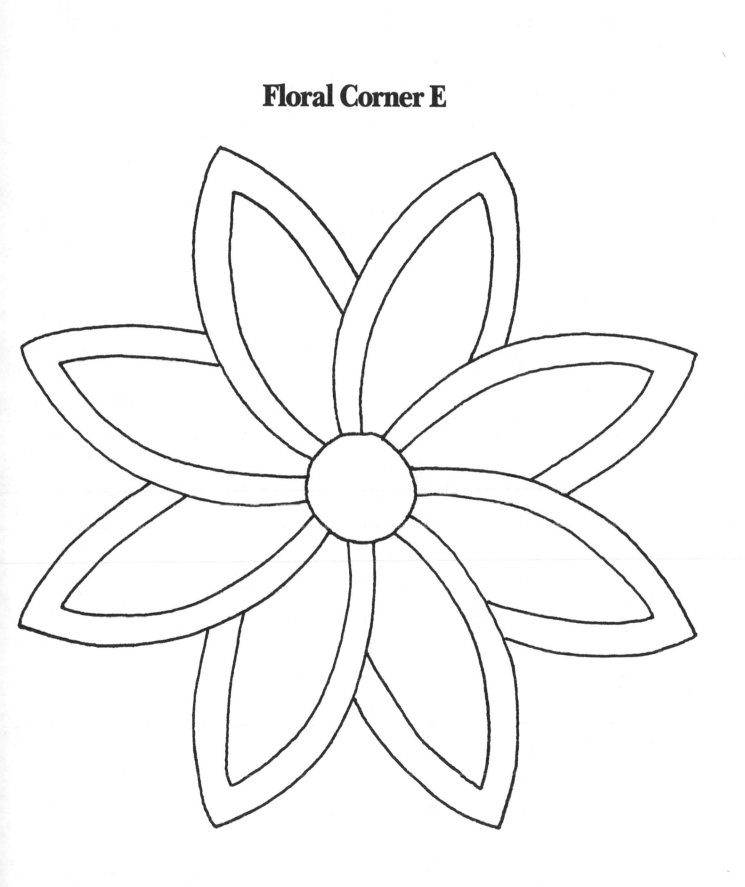

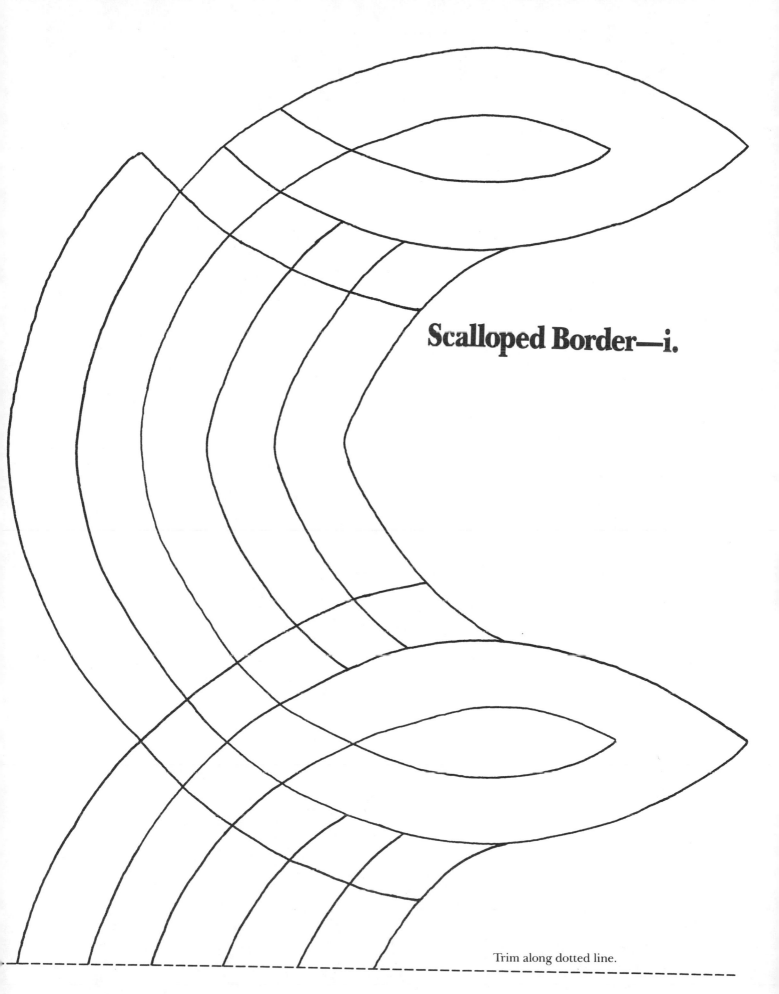

Scalloped Border—i.

Trim along dotted line.

Scalloped Border—ii.

Trim along dotted line.

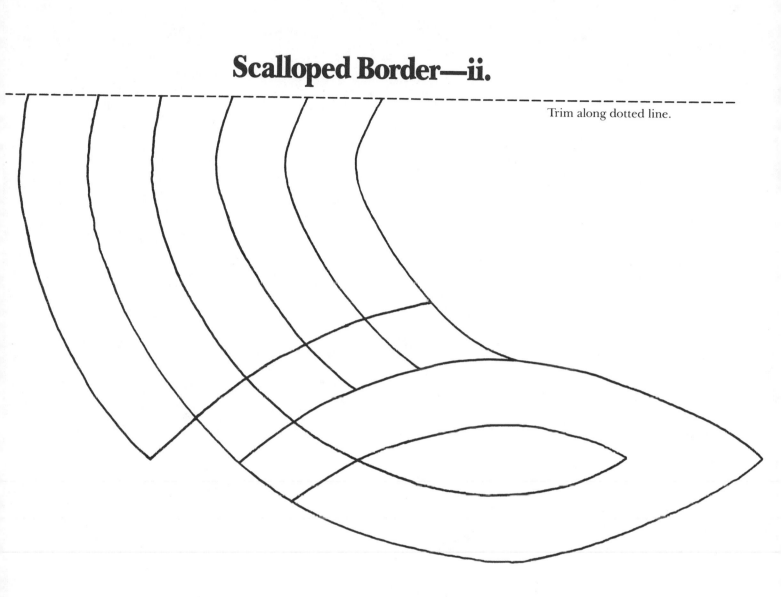

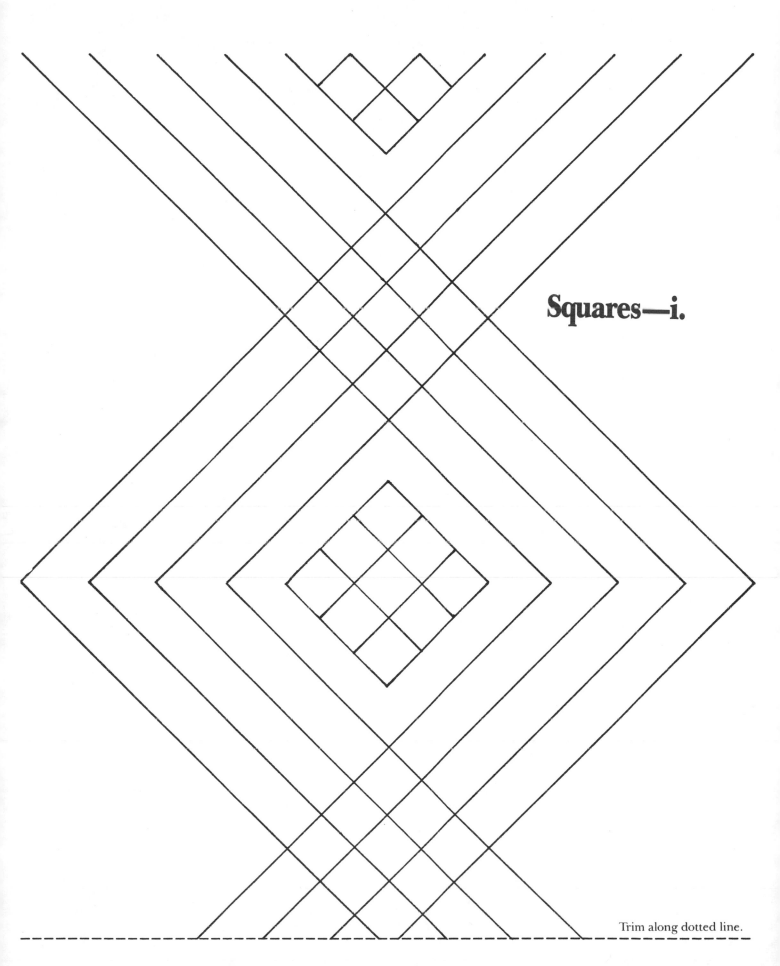

Squares—i.

Trim along dotted line.

Squares—ii.

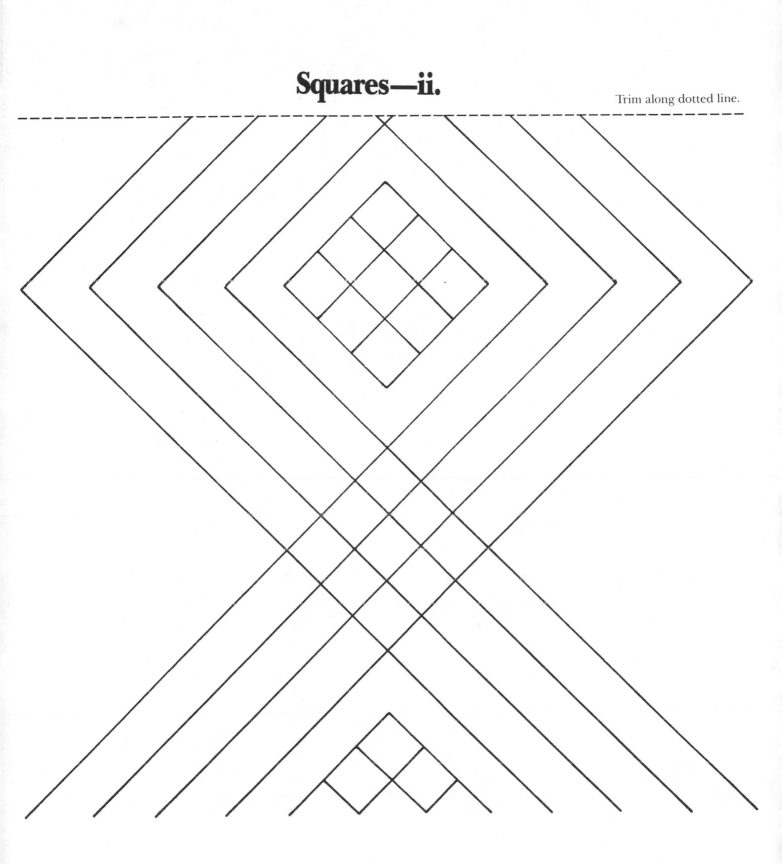

Hearts

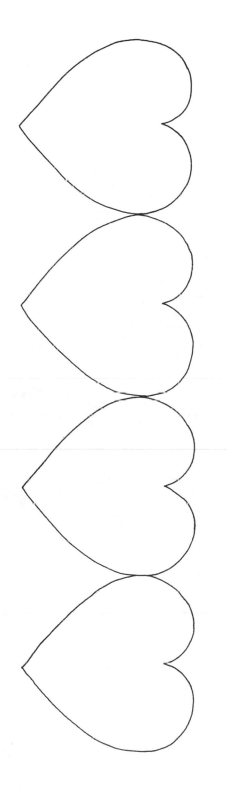

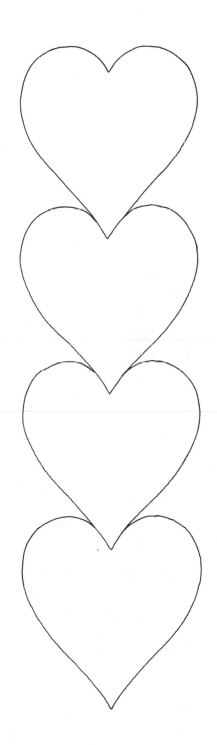

Readings and Sources

Cross Reference

Pellman, Rachel, and Kenneth Pellman. *Amish Crib Quilts*. Intercourse, Pennsylvania: Good Books, 1985.

About Antique Amish Quilts

Bishop, Robert, and Elizabeth Safanda. *A Gallery of Amish Quilts*. New York: E.P. Dutton and Company, Inc., 1976.

Haders, Phyllis. *Sunshine and Shadow: The Amish and Their Quilts*. New York: Universe Books, 1976.

Horton, Roberta. *Amish Adventure*. Lafayette, California: C&T Publishing, 1983.

Lawson, Suzy. *Amish Inspiration*. Cottage Grove, Oregon: Amity Publications, 1982.

Pellman, Rachel T. *Amish Quilt Patterns*. Intercourse, Pennsylvania: Good Books, 1984.

————, and Kenneth Pellman. *The World of Amish Quilts*. Intercourse, Pennsylvania: Good Books, 1984.

About Other Quilts

Beyer, Jinny. *Patchwork Patterns*. McLean, Virginia: EPM Publications, 1979.

Binney, Edward 3rd and Gail Binney-Winslow. *Homage to Amanda*. San Francisco: RK Press, 1984.

Bonesteel, Georgia. *More Lap Quilting With Georgia Bonesteel*. Birmingham, Alabama: Oxmoor House, Inc., 1985.

Danneman, Barbara. *Step by Step Quiltmaking*. New York: Western Publishing Company, Inc., 1975.

Finley, Ruth E. *Old Patchwork Quilts and the Women Who Made Them*. New York: Charles T. Branford Company, 1929.

Fox, Sandi. *Small Endearments: 19th Century Quilts for Children and Dolls*. Los Angeles: The Los Angeles Municipal Art Gallery Associates, 1980.

Garoutte, Sally, ed. *Uncoverings 1980*. Mill Valley, California: American Quilt Study Group, 1981.

————. *Uncoverings 1982*. Mill Valley, California: American Quilt Study Group, 1983.

Haders, Phyllis. *The Warner Collector's Guide to American Quilts*. New York: The Main Street Press, 1981.

Hall, Carrie A. and Rose G. Kretsinger. *The Romance of the Patchwork Quilt in America*. New York: Bonanza Books, 1935.

Hassel, Carla J. *You Can Be a Super Quilter!* Des Moines, Iowa: Wallace-Homestead Book Company, 1980.

Holstein, Jonathan. *The Pieced Quilt: An American Design Tradition*. Boston: New York Graphic Society, 1983.

Houck, Carter and Myron Miller. *American Quilts and How to Make Them*. New York: Charles Scribner's Sons, 1975.

Johnson, Bruce. *A Child's Comfort: Baby and Doll Quilts in American Folk Art*. New York: The Museum of American Folk Art, 1977.

Khin, Yvonne M. *The Collector's Dictionary of Quilt Names and Patterns*. Washington, D.C.: Acropolis Books, Ltd., 1980.

Kiracofe, Roderick and Michael Kile. *The Quilt Digest*. San Francisco: Kiracofe and Kile, 1983.

————. *The Quilt Digest*. San Francisco: Kiracofe and Kile, 1984.

Leone, Diana. *The Sampler Quilt*. Santa Clara, California: Leone Publications, 1980.

McCloskey, Marsha. *Wall Quilts*. Bothell, Washington: That Patchwork Place, 1983.

Murwin, Susan Aylsworth and Suzzy Chalfant Payne. *Quick and Easy Patchwork on the Sewing Machine*. New York: Dover Publications, 1979.

Orlovsky, Patsy and Myron Orlovsky. *Quilts in America*. New York: McGraw Hill Book Company, 1974.

Pellman, Rachel T. and Joanne Ranck. *Quilts Among the Plain People*. Intercourse, Pennsylvania: Good Books, 1981.

Tomlonson, Judy Schroeder. *Mennonite Quilts and Pieces*. Intercourse, Pennsylvania: Good Books, 1985.

Woodard, Thos. K. and Blanche Greenstein. *Crib Quilts and Other Small Wonders*. New York: E. P. Dutton, 1981.

About the Amish

Amish Cooking. Aylmer, Ontario: Pathway Publishing House, 1965.

Bender, H. S. *The Anabaptist Vision*. Scottdale, Pennsylvania: Herald Press, 1967.

Braght, Thieleman J. van, comp. *The Bloody Theatre; or, Martyrs Mirror*. Scottdale, Pennsylvania: Herald Press, 1951.

Budget, The. A weekly newspaper serving the Amish and Mennonite communities. Sugarcreek, Ohio, 1890—.

Devoted Christian's Prayer Book. Aylmer, Ontario: Pathway Publishing House.

Family Life. Amish periodical published monthly. Aylmer, Ontario: Pathway Publishing House.

Fisher, Sara E. and Rachel K. Stahl. *The Amish School.* Intercourse, Pennsylvania: Good Books, 1985.

Gingerich, Orland. *The Amish of Canada.* Waterloo, Ontario: Conrad Press, 1972.

Good, Merle. *Who Are the Amish?* Intercourse, Pennsylvania: Good Books, 1985.

——, and Phyllis Pellman Good. *20 Most Asked Questions About the Amish and Mennonites.* Intercourse, Pennsylvania: Good Books, 1979.

Good, Phyllis Pellman and Rachel Thomas Pellman. *From Amish and Mennonite Kitchens.* Intercourse, Pennsylvania: Good Books, 1984.

Hostetler, John A. *Amish Life.* Scottdale, Pennsylvania: Herald Press, 1959.

——. *Amish Society.* Baltimore: Johns Hopkins University Press, 1963.

——, and Gertrude E. Huntingdon. *Children in Amish Society.* New York: Holt, Rhinehart and Winston, Inc., 1971.

Keim, Albert N. *Compulsory Education and the Amish.* Boston: Beacon Press, 1975.

Klaassen, Walter. *Anabaptism: Neither Catholic Nor Protestant.* Waterloo, Ontario: Conrad Press, 1972.

Ruth, John L. *A Quiet and Peaceable Life.* Intercourse, Pennsylvania: Good Books, 1985.

Scott, Stephen. *Plain Buggies—Amish, Mennonite and Brethren Horse-Drawn Transportation.* Intercourse, Pennsylvania: Good Books, 1981.

——. *Why Do They Dress That Way?* Intercourse, Pennsylvania: Good Books, 1985.

Nine-Patch, c. 1885. Cotton, 31 × 38. Holmes Co., Ohio. Sandra Mitchell.

Index

"Amish" patterns, 8
BACHELOR'S PUZZLE, 72
BARS, 20
BASKETS (pattern), 36
Baskets (quilting template), 107
Basket with Tulip, 101–103
Batting, 11
BEAR PAW, 56
Binding, 11
Borders, 11, 12, 15
BOW TIE, 46
Buying fabric, 8

Cable, 93–95
CAROLINA LILY, 54
CENTER DIAMOND, 16
Choosing fabrics, 8
Choosing patterns, 8
Circular Feather, 77
Clamshell, 117
Color, 8, 9
CROWN OF THORNS, 51

DIAGONAL TRIANGLES, 67
Diamond, 111
Displaying quilts, 12
Dogwood, 99
Double Irish Chain, 24
DOUBLE T, 30
DOUBLE WEDDING RING, 64

DRUNKARD'S PATH, 68

FAN, 38
Fan, 101, 111
Feather Border, 83
Feather Heart with Cross-Hatching, 109
Fiddlehead Fern, 89–91
Floral Border Design, 99
Floral Corner, 81, 87, 91, 105–107, 113
Four-Patch (Double), 23
Fruit, 105

GARDEN MAZE, 60
Grapes with Leaves, 97

Hearts, 123

IRISH CHAIN (Double), 24
IRISH CHAIN (Single), 25
Ivy Leaf, 87

JACOB'S LADDER, 34

Leaves, 103
LOG CABIN, 26
Lone Star, 32

Making templates, 9
Marking (patches), 9–10
Marking (quilting patterns), 10
Mitering borders, 11–12
MONKEY WRENCH, 52
MULTIPLE PATCH, 22

Nine-Patch (Double), 22
OCEAN WAVES, 40

Piecing, 10
PINWHEEL, 58
Pumpkin Seed, 99

Quilting, 10–11

RAIL FENCE, 29
RAILROAD CROSSING, 62
ROBBING PETER TO PAY PAUL, 48
ROLLING STONE, 74
ROMAN STRIPE, 42

Scalloped Border, 115–117
SHOO-FLY, 50
Single Irish Chain, 25
Squares, 119–121
STARS, 32
SUNSHINE AND SHADOW, 18

TREE OF LIFE, 70
Triangular Rose, 79
Tulip, 93, 97
TUMBLING BLOCKS, 44

Variations, 12

Yardage, 8

About the Author

Rachel Thomas Pellman is manager of The Old Country Store in Intercourse, Pennsylvania, which features quilts, crafts, and toys made by more than 250 Amish and Mennonite craftspersons. A graduate of Eastern Mennonite College, she and her husband Kenneth have written THE WORLD OF AMISH QUILTS and AMISH CRIB QUILTS. She has also co-authored QUILTS AMONG THE PLAIN PEOPLE, FROM AMISH AND MENNONITE KITCHENS, and 12 Pennsylvania Dutch Cookbooks.

Rachel and Kenneth share an interest in folk art and crafts, and the interpretation of their people. Kenneth is manager of The People's Place, an educational center concerned with Amish and Mennonite arts, faith, and culture.

The Pellmans were married in 1976. They live in Lancaster, Pennsylvania, with their two young sons, Nathaniel and Jesse. They are members of the Rossmere Mennonite Church.